SO-AHI-895

24TH&GLORY

DIRK CHATELAIN

BOB
DOZER

RON
BOONE

JOHNNY
RODGERS

BOB
GIBSON

ROGER
SAYERS

GALE
SAYERS

MARLIN
BRISCOE

Working Together to Tell
Nebraska's African-American History

A SPORTSWRITER KNOWS that the game is more than a game. Sometimes a lot more.

The men profiled here are some of the greatest athletes Nebraska has ever produced, and they grew up in the same neighborhood and generation. That's a good story in itself, but there's more. As African Americans coming of age during the Civil Rights Movement, their lives reflect larger issues. Their stories form a portrait of Omaha's black community during those crucial years.

Brownville, 1864, the earliest known photo of African-Americans in Nebraska.

History Nebraska (aka the Nebraska State Historical Society) was eager to partner with the Omaha World-Herald to publish this book. We look at the big picture: how Nebraska statehood was shaped by the racial politics of the Civil War; how black homesteaders sought new beginnings on the prairies; how the Great Migration built African American communities in our largest cities; how local activists challenged Northern-style segregation.

These and other stories are told in our publications, at the Nebraska History Museum in Lincoln, and on our website. We preserve and share black history through artifacts, photos, historical markers and the collections of our library and archives. Search "African American" at history.nebraska.gov to learn more and follow History Nebraska on social media to keep up with events and educational programming.

There's so much more to be told, and this book represents an important new chapter. And it's also simply a great read, so vivid you'll feel as if you've met the people and walked along 24th Street in the 1950s and 1960s, witnessing for yourself all of that era's injustice, hope and glory. As a work of history and journalism — and as a page-turner as exciting as a close game — we are pleased to endorse 24th & Glory.

Trevor Jones, Director/CEO
History Nebraska

History NEBRASKA

*Above: Students await
Bob Gibson, Oct. 17, 1964.*

*Title page: Aerial of Logan
Fontenelle homes in 1947.*

Cover illustration by Matt Haney

Copyright 2019 Omaha World-Herald.
All rights reserved.

No part of this book may be reproduced,
stored in a retrieval system, or transmitted
in any form or by any means, electronic,
mechanical, photocopying, recording or
otherwise, without prior consent of the
publisher, the Omaha World-Herald.

Omaha World-Herald
1314 Douglas St.
Omaha, NE 68102-1811
omaha.com | owhstore.com

First Edition, Third Printing
ISBN: 978-1-7322317-5-7
Printed by Walsworth Publishing Co.

Omaha's Near North Side Landmarks

The neighborhood covered roughly two square miles and contained almost all of Omaha's black population. As a result, the best athletes lived in striking proximity to each other and to North Omaha cultural cornerstones.

A *Intersection of 24th & Lake Streets, the heart of North Omaha*

B *Kountze Park: 3505 Florence Blvd.*

C *Bryant Center: 24th & Burdette Streets*

D *Omaha Star: 2216 N. 24th St.*

E *Burdette Field: North 21st & Burdette Streets*

F *Jewell Building: 2221 N. 24th St.*

G *First site of Near North YMCA: 2213 Lake St.*

H *Near North YMCA Building: 2311 N. 22nd St.*

I *Kellom School: 1311 N. 24th St.*

J *Horace Mann School: 3720 Florence Blvd.*

K *Howard Kennedy School: 2906 N. 30th St.*

L *Tech High School: 3215 Cuming St.*

M *Skeet's BBQ: 2201 N. 24th St.*

N *Fair Deal Cafe: 2118 N. 24th St.*

O *Bob Boozer Residence: 2402 N. 25th St.*

P *Lothrop School: 3300 N. 22nd St.*

Q *Central High School: 124 N. 20th St.*

R *Goodwin's Spencer Street Barber Shop: 3116 N. 24th St.*

S *Logan Fontenelle Housing Project: 20th to 24th Streets; Paul to Clark Streets*

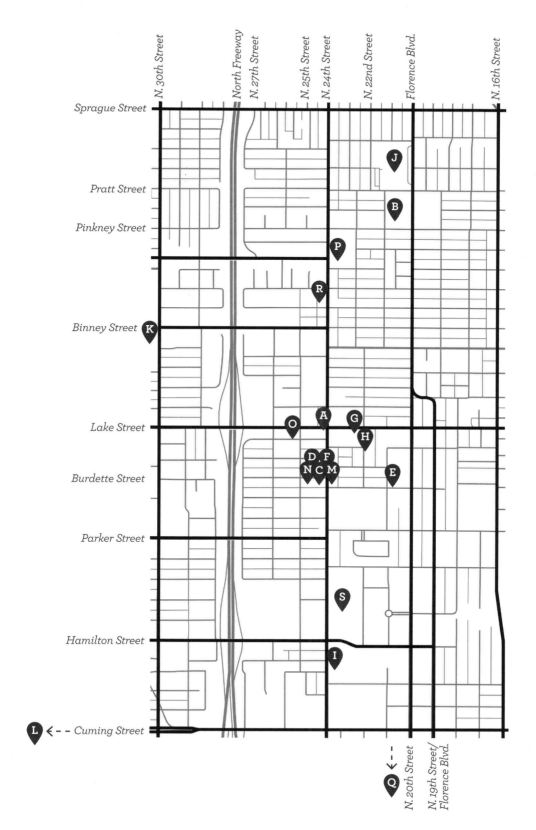

Echoes of '68

NOBODY TOLD THE MAN on the mound.

Not his teammates in the St. Louis Cardinals dugout. Not 54,692 fans at Busch Stadium. Certainly not the hopeless Detroit Tigers.

As the ninth inning began, everyone saw Bob Gibson inching closer to baseball immortality ... except Gibson.

The 32-year-old from Omaha stood alone atop 15 inches of dirt, the most dominant force in America's most popular sport, a source of universal amazement against a backdrop of national turbulence.

Across America that Wednesday afternoon — Oct. 2, 1968 — barbers and shopkeepers cranked up their radios. Doctors and lawyers postponed appointments. Kids rushed home from school and switched their black-and-white TVs to NBC, where Harry Caray delivered play-by-play.

"All over the world," Caray said, "people I'm sure are tense as they are here at the ballpark for this pitch."

Yet Gibson, who'd already thrown 130 pitches, wasn't in on the secret.

He breathed heavily in 82-degree sunshine, his mouth slightly open. He squinted beneath his hat, the bill lopsided and wavy like a rotten wood floor. His red wool sweatshirt bled through his white sweat-soaked jersey, No. 45.

He nodded to his catcher, folded his hands to his chest and unleashed a delivery defined by power, grace and fury. His left leg landed and his right leg swung so hard across his body that he nearly fell over — like a tetherball whipping around its pole. Gibson finished 5 feet left of the mound as Al Kaline whiffed at a two-seam fastball on the outside corner.

"Got him! Listen to the crowd!"

Gibson still didn't understand the commotion. He took off his cap, wiped his forehead with his sore right forearm and stepped back to the mound. When he looked up, his catcher stood in front of home plate, pointing to an outfield scoreboard.

Let's go, Gibson motioned — he hated to wait. Finally, he turned and saw the message.

Gibson has tied World Series record for strikeouts in a single game with his 15th.

All year, the two-time World Series MVP had focused amid chaos. A day after Martin Luther King Jr. was buried, Gibson opened the '68 season allowing one run in seven innings. The day Bobby Kennedy died, he hurled his first shutout. Four days after the Democratic National Convention riots in Chicago, he pitched 10 scoreless innings, won his 20th game and dropped his ERA to 0.99.

Bob Gibson's dominance on display in Game 1 of the 1968 World Series.

Gibson wasn't the only North Omahan on the sports page.

That first week of October, one native son led the NFL in rushing. Another averaged 22 points per game in the NBA. One was about to begin a 17,000-point pro basketball career. Another was about to break football's most stubborn racial barrier. One — a future Heisman Trophy winner — broke Friday night records.

They all came from the same parks and gyms. The same schools and coaches.

Their fathers shared the stench of the kill floors. Their mothers shared the pews at Zion Baptist Church. On North 24th Street, they rode the same streetcars, visited the same comic book stores and tasted the same Skeet's barbecue pork — who else applied hot sauce with a paintbrush?

They knew each other like cousins. They cheered Gibson, too.

Back in St. Louis, Tigers cleanup hitter Norm Cash fouled back a fastball and the crowd urged it out of play. The Cardinals' 4-0 lead was safe. Fans wanted strikeouts, not pop-ups.

"It is such a dramatic scene," Caray said, "that I find myself not wanting to say a word because your picture is telling you the whole story."

But the picture wasn't complete. Not even close.

Echoes of '68

The Omaha World-Herald Top 100 Athletes

In 2015, The World-Herald ranked Nebraska's Top 100 athletes of all-time. Four of the top five came from the same neighborhood in the 1950s and '60s.

 **#1 BOB GIBSON**

Tech High
1953 graduate

 #2 GALE SAYERS

Central High
1961 graduate

 #4 BOB BOOZER

Tech High
1955 graduate

 #5 JOHNNY RODGERS

Tech High
1969 graduate

 #17 MARLIN BRISCOE

South High
1963 graduate

#26 RON BOONE

Tech High
1964 graduate

 #36 ROGER SAYERS

Central High
1960 graduate

Down in the Cardinals clubhouse, hate mail littered Gibson's locker. "Why don't you and the other blackbirds on the Cardinals move to Africa where you belong." Above the letters, a button proclaimed Gibson's worldview: "I'm not prejudiced; I hate everyone."

Half a mile east of Busch Stadium, civil rights protesters marched beneath the new Gateway Arch. A single-engine plane tugged a banner promoting segregationist George Wallace for president.

And back in North Omaha, Gibson's old neighborhood ripped apart, brick by brick. He could baffle the world's best hitters. He couldn't save the culture that raised him.

On his 139th pitch, Gibson's 2-2 slider curled in on Cash's swinging hands.

"Got him!"

The crowd roared for the record. Gibson didn't crack a smile. He didn't even step off the mound. It was Game 1 of the 1968 Fall Classic and the Cardinals needed one more out.

The last Tiger at bat was Willie Horton. With two strikes, Gibson took a deep breath, filling his cheeks. He raised his hands, kicked his leg. His left arm flailed, his right hand spun a slider that started so far inside that Horton thought it was going to hit him. The ball turned back over the corner.

"Struck him out! Look at the scene on the field!"

Look at the scene 50 years later. Gibson's 17 strikeouts still stand in the record book — probably forever. But here in his hometown, a bigger story drifts away ...

The secret of Nebraska's greatest generation of athletes.

They rose out of segregation — higher and higher — as racial tensions in North O boiled hotter and hotter.

During the civil rights era, seven ascended to national prominence:

Bob Boozer, the sweet-shooting gentle giant who chased Negro League buses down Erskine Street before he chased basketballs at the Near North YMCA, earned an Olympic gold medal and NBA championship ring.

Gale and Roger Sayers, the nomadic brothers, ran circles around defenses while living out of boxes. Gale became the youngest Hall of Famer in pro football history. Roger settled for a summer as the world's fastest man.

Marlin Briscoe, the undersized quarterback who whipped spirals at a birch tree in the housing projects, jumped from small-college magician to Denver Broncos rookie starting quarterback to Pro Bowl wide receiver to Super Bowl champ.

Ron Boone, who grew up on a dead-end street with 60 kids and bloomed late at an outdoor basketball paradise named Bryant Center, finished third all-time in American Basketball Association scoring.

Johnny Rodgers, the son of a 14-year-old mother who, before he eluded Oklahoma Sooners in the Game of the Century, learned to escape a vicious rooster en route to his backyard outhouse.

Of course, Gibson was the best of all. Blessed and burdened with fury, he might have wasted his gifts if his oldest brother hadn't come home from war and rescued him from rebellion.

Cardinals catcher Tim McCarver clasps the pitching hand of Bob Gibson moments after Gibson's 17th strikeout in Game 1 of the 1968 World Series.

Their paths are distinct, but their origin is the same: a neighborhood so vibrant, so unified that individual accomplishments and devastations touched every house from Tech High to Kountze Park.

A neighborhood where kids had freedom to roam and discover their passions, but if they stepped out of line — look out! — strangers lined up to swat their butts. "We had like 900 mothers," one said.

A neighborhood where proximity to social, religious and economic hot spots resembled a village. Most landmarks didn't just lie within walking distance but shouting distance.

A neighborhood where, depending on the night, kids might see Martin Luther King Jr., Malcolm X, Ray Charles, James Brown, Chuck Berry, Joe Louis, Satchel Paige, Jesse Owens, Jackie Robinson, Oscar Robertson or O.J. Simpson — just walking down 24th Street.

A neighborhood where even the street hustlers respected a "code of ethics" to develop and protect the most talented athletes, for they were the best chance to inspire pride.

A neighborhood created by racism but fortified economically by packinghouse workers who came home coated in blood. No wonder they filled the bars on Friday nights.

A neighborhood that, despite its humble size and remote location in middle America, became a progressive beacon in the national protest movement, recognized by would-be presidents and would-be revolutionaries.

Omaha's black athletes of the 1950s and '60s were driven by ruthless, tireless mentors; nurtured by a fanatical rec sports culture; sharpened by hundreds of talented peers, most of whom didn't become famous.

They endured the sting of scholarship quotas, unjust referee whistles and a maddening paradox: Strangers wanted their autographs but refused to be their neighbors.

Together in triumph, they put North Omaha on the sports map. Together in heartbreak, they watched it burn. The neighborhood of their youth — this breeding ground for brilliance — didn't survive the 1960s.

The story has been shared only in pieces. It spans more than a century, from Omaha's dirtiest days through the baby boom, culminating with one glorious Sunday in October 1968 — four days after Gibson's 17 strikeouts. In a span of two hours that afternoon:

- Bob Gibson recorded an MLB record seventh consecutive World Series win, all complete games.
- Marlin Briscoe became the first black quarterback to start a professional football game.
- Gale Sayers dazed the mighty Baltimore Colts with a breathtaking 59-yard touchdown run; he called it the best of his career.

How did the stars line up? Genetic luck? Cosmic coincidence? Or a set of variables more complicated than speed, strength and desire?

Kids had a blast at Omaha's Logan Fontenelle housing projects in the 1940s and 1950s.

"It was something in the dirt," said Preston Love Jr., the former Nebraska football player and son of North Omaha's legendary jazz musician.

Time threatens to erase the tracks. One by one Omaha loses its heroes of October 1968. Their voices fade. Their memories dim. But the truth endures.

Before color TV and air conditioning, before wrecking balls leveled factories and bulldozers demolished houses, before police officers killed unarmed teenagers and a bomb killed a cop, before black leaders moved away and black children moved inside, before the 24th and Lake crowds went silent, North Omaha had a system. An ethos. A rhythm.

Put your ear to the street. You can still hear the echo.

Echoes of '68

Chapter 1

Coach Gibson

HE WALKED TO THE open field behind the old brick school, wrapped his big hands around his shovel and stabbed the ground. Lifted the dirt and dumped it nearby. Packed it and reached for another load.

North Omaha's athletic pinnacle was still two decades away, but it started when a World War II vet built a place to stand, right off Paul Street, 1947.

Scoop. Dump. Pack.

At 26 years old, Josh Gibson was a great athlete himself. He had shoulders like fence posts, a tuba for a voice and a snap-quick temper. What Bob's big brother didn't have was a role in his hometown. Not yet.

South of his shovel, downtown Omaha landmarks loomed a mile away. The Woolworth and Brandeis stores. Hotels Paxton and Fontenelle. Places he didn't go. But to his north, the world was free and alive.

You could walk the side streets and hear Ella Fitzgerald crooning from front-porch radios as chickens and ducks scurried around backyards. See kids hurry to Kellom School's dirt basketball courts — dribbling got a lot easier when they finally poured concrete.

When you reached the bricks of 24th Street, streetcar wires stretched from wooden poles like spiderwebs. Trolleys carried beef luggers and hotel maids past storefront windows marked with daily sales. Fresh pastries wafted out of Jewish bakeries and onto the sidewalk, competing with the ever-present scent of Omaha's perfume — downright potent when the south wind blew.

Manure.

Past the jitney stands and meat markets, church steeples and synagogues, doctors and lawyers offices. In just one mile of 24th — from Cuming to Ohio Streets — you could count 170 businesses, their signs competing for attention like kids at Mama's feet. Seven tailors, seven cigar shops, 12 beauty shops, 13 grocery stores, 16 restaurants and so many taverns, where crowds spilled into the streets for the occasional fistfight.

Play nine ball at Jimmy Jewell's. Eat chitlins at DeWitt's. Listen to 78s at Allen's Record Shop. Poke your head into Federal Market, where families charged groceries and paid up at week's end — Mr. Lewis kept stacks of IOUs.

Squint under the sparkling marquee of the Ritz Theatre with its sticky floors and greasy popcorn — no wonder they called it the "bug house." Put on your suit and squeeze into the Dreamland Ballroom, where jazz and blues orchestras — sweating in their white tuxedos — bounced beats off the walls, sometimes toting their horns right out the door, down the staircase, into the street and back up to the stage, blaring the whole way.

The intersection of 24th and Lake Streets looking south in 1947. At the time, 170 businesses operated along 24th from Cuming to Ohio Streets.

At the 24-hour Snack Stop cafe, sit at the table where Nat King Cole wrote his first hit single, "Straighten Up and Fly Right." At the Omaha Star, get weekly reports on civil rights protests, local church sermons and a Brooklyn Dodgers rookie first baseman named Jackie Robinson.

Ahhh, now we're getting somewhere.

To spearhead an epic sports movement, a bustling 24th Street isn't enough. You need inspiration and drive. Talent, time and one tenacious coach.

The Federal Market at 1414 N. 24th St. around 1946.

When Josh Gibson stuck his shovel in the schoolyard in 1947, he didn't just build a pitcher's mound, he reshaped a neighborhood.

Coach Gibson

***

Let's dig a little deeper. 1859.

A Republican presidential candidate stands atop a bluff and looks across the Missouri River at a hodgepodge of sod huts, saloons and stores. Abe Lincoln didn't bother crossing the water.

After Lincoln won the White House, Omaha transformed from a frontier outpost into a

Omaha looking northwest from 13th and Farnam Streets in 1865.

primitive version of Las Vegas — without the lights. A Kansas City writer described its northern neighbor as a "cesspool of iniquity, for it is given up to lawlessness and is overrun with a horde of fugitives from justice and dangerous men of all kinds who carry things with a high hand and a loose rein. ... If you want to find a rogue's rookery, go to Omaha."

What cleansed the city and made its citizens rich? Dead cattle. In the 1880s, Omaha became synonymous with stockyards, packinghouses and immigrant labor.

M.O. Ricketts

South Omaha divided into ethnic neighborhoods. The Near North Side was more like the city's foyer. Germans, Swedes, Danes and Irish entered first. Once they got comfortable and saved up money, they sought better housing west and north of downtown. Italians and Jews followed through the revolving doors. The latter, especially, built businesses on 24th Street.

Blacks first arrived before the Civil War and moved into the foyer. By the new century, they were lawyers, engineers, dentists, brick masons. Mostly, they were welcome. Whites patronized black businesses. They helped vote M.O. Ricketts, Omaha's first black doctor, into the State Legislature. Prejudice and discrimination existed, but it rarely led to confrontation.

That all changed with beetles and bullets.

In 1915-16, boll weevils infested Southern cotton fields, prompting landowners to reduce wages or fire workers. Where could blacks find work? It wasn't Birmingham or Atlanta, where Jim Crow locked them out of jobs. It was Chicago and Cleveland, Pittsburgh and Detroit, Kansas City and Omaha.

Northern factories faced a labor problem during World War I. Their workers left assembly lines for Europe, and Uncle Sam closed the immigration spigot.

So factories published ads in black newspapers. Railroad porters spread stories of opportunity. Across the South, visions of a promised land took seed in black barbershops and flowered in black churches. Let's go where they have real schools and ballot boxes. Entire congregations migrated to Omaha from towns like Evergreen, Alabama. They were pioneers and — in cases when the Ku Klux Klan threatened them — refugees.

Omaha's black population more than doubled from 1910 to 1920 — from 4,425 to 10,315. The surge didn't go unnoticed. Whites felt threatened, especially when the war ended and soldiers returned home to find blacks occupying their old jobs.

Will Brown

Tensions flared in the summer of 1919. In September, they exploded. A 19-year-old white woman in South Omaha claimed that a black man had jumped out of the bushes, assaulted her disabled friend and raped her. Police arrested a migrant packinghouse worker named Will Brown, who had rheumatism and struggled to move.

Two days later, a Sunday afternoon, teenagers made an impromptu march from Bancroft School to the new Douglas County Courthouse, where Brown was held on the sixth floor.

By 5:30 p.m., the crowd had swelled to about 5,000 and a riot began. Protesters heaved bricks through windows and fired guns into the air. As night fell, they started the courthouse ablaze and ripped ladders and hoses from the arriving firemen. Guards rushed prisoners to the roof, where they lay flat to avoid gunfire.

When Mayor Ed Smith tried to defuse the madness, the crowd mashed his head with a baseball bat and strung him up to a light pole before officers rescued him.

At 10:30 p.m., rioters finally reached the black man in blue overalls. They fired a dozen shots into Will Brown's body.

Rioters scale the walls of the Douglas County Courthouse amid racial tensions in September 1919.

Coach Gibson

In September 1919, white rioters gawk at Will Brown's body (not shown), which burns in front of them.

They carried him down to the street, where he was stripped, bludgeoned and castrated, then hanged from a light pole and riddled with more bullets. They dragged the corpse through the streets before burning it atop a wood pyre at 17th and Dodge Streets. A young boy sold bits of the rope that hanged Will Brown for 10 cents apiece.

Meanwhile, hundreds of blacks heard about the furor and fled across the Missouri River. As rioters prepared to march toward 24th and Lake Streets, a rumor stopped them: *Federal troops are coming!*

The mob melted into the night.

The next day, 800 troops from Fort Omaha fortified 24th and Lake Streets with machine guns. Police arrested hundreds of rioters, but not one was convicted of murder or sentenced to lengthy jail time.

"Omaha was disgraced and humiliated ..." wrote World-Herald editor Harvey Newbranch in a Pulitzer Prize-winning editorial. "Should the day ever come when jungle rule becomes dominant ... the God who rules us would turn His face in sorrow."

The consequences of the courthouse riot rippled across Omaha for years, decades, generations. Will Brown was a powerless packinghouse worker. He was nobody. But on the Near North Side, he became a symbol of everybody. *This is what can happen.*

Reminders kept coming. In early 1925, the KKK was at the peak of its power when hooded Klansmen visited the Omaha home of a Baptist minister and black nationalist. Earl Little was out of town, but his pregnant wife stepped outside and received a threat. Klansmen busted her windows with the butts of their rifles.

One year later, the Littles left Omaha in fear with their four children, the youngest of whom was just learning to talk. His parents named him Malcolm. The world would know him as Malcolm X.

From the Great Migration and the Great War, a ghastly murder and nights of terror, Omaha's half-century of de facto segregation was born.

The city couldn't shut out blacks. It could, however, lock the foyer. Exclude blacks from moving west and north like the European immigrants did. Deny home mortgages and insurance policies outside the Near North Side. Prohibit admission to restaurants and theaters and swimming pools and skating rinks and, most importantly, white schools.

Blacks weren't the only residents of the Near North Side. In fact, the area was majority white until the 1950s — poor and working class. But those whites were free to patronize Florence or Dundee. Free to move elsewhere. Free to aspire. Blacks were largely confined to the box.

Cuming Street marked the south border, 30th Street the west. The northern line blurred over time, eventually reaching Ames Avenue. And the eastern edge? Sixteenth Street.

Two square miles — with one iconic intersection.

***

Come a little closer to the surface. June 1938.

The night started like a church service. Crowds packed the bars at 24th and Lake Streets, turning their ears to radios. *Shhhh ...*

At Yankee Stadium in New York, a black icon stepped into the ring to face his nemesis. Joe Louis had lost once to German Max Schmeling, a defeat that crushed black communities across America and emboldened Nazi ruler Adolf Hitler.

But the boxers met again in '38 and Louis got revenge. Three knockdowns in the first two minutes. When the referee stopped the fight, North Omaha bars emptied. Houses emptied. Twenty-fourth and Lake resembled Times Square, with 2,500 blacks celebrating in the street.

They crashed bottles, climbed poles, detached trolleys from the tracks, started bonfires. When police arrived via motorcycles, they danced a ring around the law. For 2½ hours, the logjam didn't budge.

Joe Louis in 1936.

The boldest of them hurled crates and stones — even a washtub — from rooftops. One car inched through the crowd with a large box shaped like a coffin and decorated with red paper, a swastika and a message.

"Here lies Max."

That's the kind of fervor North Omaha felt for a black athlete it didn't even know. Imagine their reaction if they'd realized a future baseball MVP was sleeping five blocks away.

Bob Gibson was 2 years old that summer. His parents, Pack and Victoria, met in a Louisiana church. In the 1920s, they moved to Lincoln and ultimately Omaha. Pack worked on FDR's New Deal construction crews. He built a pulpit at Morningstar Baptist Church, where he was a trustee.

But in June 1935, Pack died from a form of tuberculosis, leaving his wife with six kids and another in the womb. Pack Robert Gibson Jr. arrived on Nov. 9, full of spunk but devoid of security.

Victoria worked at a laundromat and cleaned houses but couldn't satisfy seven mouths. When holes opened in Robert's shoes, he slipped cardboard in the bottom so his feet wouldn't get wet. On Maple Street, in a two-bedroom rental, the family covered holes in the floor with tin cans. One night a rat wiggled through, climbed up an army cot and bit Robert's ear. He never forgot.

He suffered from rickets disease, but his biggest problem was breathing. At 3, Robert fell ill with asthma or perhaps pneumonia. He was wrapped in a quilt, carried to the hospital and told that if he got back on his feet he'd receive a gift. A new baseball glove.

Josh Gibson, pictured here in 1939, was a standout athlete at Omaha Tech.

Who made such a promise? His oldest brother, his father figure, a 17-year-old named Leroy. North Omaha knew him as Josh.

He shined on Omaha Tech's track and field team and in city baseball leagues, but after his dad died Josh considered dropping out and working full time — most blacks didn't make it through high school anyway. His mom encouraged him to stay. Josh graduated from Tech in 1939 and wanted to attend college.

Instead, at 19, he went to work at the packinghouse, a path that could've been a career until Japan bombed Pearl Harbor. In 1943, the oldest Gibson son went off to war. Josh took charge of Army softball and basketball teams and learned that America wasn't the only place that scorned black men — people in India thought that he had a tail.

Back home, his family was escaping the rats.

***

"A Cinderella transformation of a shabby Omaha residential district."

That's how The World-Herald described one of America's first public housing projects.

Urban housing had been a national disaster since the Industrial Revolution. In Eastern cities, shanties and slums followed the factory boom, producing cesspools of crime and disease.

The New Deal provided public money for 50 housing projects. Omaha surprised big city competitors by landing two. The second, Southside Terrace, stretched atop mostly empty hills overlooking the South Omaha stockyards. The first, Logan Fontenelle, opened in December 1937 and replaced the rat traps north of downtown.

Named after a local Indian chief, Logan Fontenelle started with 29 one- and two-story brick buildings, containing 284 family apartments. It featured bright kitchens with table-top gas stoves and electric refrigerators. Even furnaces. A new city park and two recreation centers divided the new subsidized neighborhood.

The Public Works Administration, The World-Herald reported, was the "fairy godmother" whose $2 million federal grant was the "magic wand." Applications were so competitive that another 272 units were built. Initially, most residents were white.

In '43, Bob Gibson's family moved to the black section of Logan Fontenelle between 22nd and 24th Streets.

Sure, there were administrative headaches. Cracking plaster. Noisy neighbors. Fights between blacks and whites. One resident complained that he couldn't find his front door because they all looked the same. A more serious issue was tenants turning down good jobs because their salaries would be too high for the projects.

But in the 1940s, Logan Fontenelle represented progress.

Logan Fontenelle opened in December 1937. This view of five-room units is from 22nd and Paul Streets. The projects nearly doubled in size in proceeding years.

Housing Projects

The best way to land one free housing project in the depths of the Great Depression? Shoot for two.

That was Philip Klutznick's strategy as he rode the rails to Washington, D.C., in October 1933, four months after FDR signed the National Industrial Recovery Act.

The New Deal program authorized $100 million in federal funds for slum clearance and low-rent housing projects. Cities didn't even have to match Washington's funding. What a deal. Of course, the government had money for only 50 projects, and every major American city — wrecked by the Depression — wanted a slice of economic stimulus.

Klutznick, a 1930 Creighton Law School grad and city employee, had his work cut out. He wrote grants for two sites: one in North Omaha, one in South Omaha. In Washington, he presented photos of Omaha's most dilapidated neighborhoods and unveiled architectural

drawings of "neat, little cottages which no one would ever think of building in connection with a slum clearance and multiple public housing program," as Klutznick wrote. To his surprise, Omaha went 2 for 2.

Klutznick, who wrote state legislation creating the Omaha Housing Authority, later served in seven U.S. presidential administrations, rising to Jimmy Carter's secretary of commerce.

But in Omaha, his shining moment came May 23, 1937, when the city broke ground on its first housing project at 22nd and Paul Streets. Those brick cottages became anchors in North and South Omaha — and home to many of the city's best athletes.

Logan Fontenelle was a beehive of activity, particularly when the weather turned warm. Here, a parade line of kids — both black and white — winds through the housing project.

On warm days, the courtyards buzzed with kids. You might see future actor John Beasley coming down from 26th and Caldwell Streets, where he lived. Or little Cathy Hughes, who'd one day start a media empire and become the second-richest black woman in America (behind Oprah). Isaiah Davis would help NASA engineer space shuttles, and brother Herbie became Omaha's first black battalion fire chief. Preston Love Jr., who would manage Jesse Jackson's 1984 early presidential campaign, watched the older kids in awe.

"I'm the guy they took the basketball from and said, 'Go home little boy,'" Love said. "I'd go home crying."

Just be careful crossing the sidewalks. That's where Bob Gibson and his friends ran laps around the buildings. "Like thundering horses," Love said.

Bob was a bucking colt. His uncle frequently offered him a dime if he could sit still for five minutes, knowing he'd never have to pay. Bob traded away Josh's high school track medals. He lit brother Richard's model planes on fire. At school, he pulled girls' hair and hurled paper wads, then hid the teacher's notes directed to his mom.

Of course, Bob wasn't the only ornery one.

On Lake Street, an open bakery window at street level offered the perfect heist. Older brother Fred Gibson and his friends lifted Bob by his ankles and dangled him through the window, where he reached down to a basement counter and grabbed the goodies. If Bob did his job, they were running free — fresh doughnuts in hand — before the baker noticed.

He wasn't always so lucky. Once Gibson and his best friend, Rodney Wead, sneaked out of the bushes and hit the lever on a streetcar at 28th and Lake Streets, causing it to stop. Word got back to their mothers.

"They beat our butts right on 24th Street," said Wead, about 11 at the time. "One had a strap. One had a switch. The guys teased us about that forever."

Bob could ignore his buddies. He couldn't hide from Josh, who came home from India with an honorable discharge and heard of little brother's mischief. It was time for a crackdown.

***

By any modern standard, Josh Gibson should've coached at a local high school. Won state championships. Sent kids off to college. That's what he wanted as he pursued a teaching degree at Omaha University after the war.

But Omaha Public Schools didn't hire black secondary teachers or coaches. In May '47, Superintendent Harry Burke told blacks during a meeting at Zion Baptist that "there had been no vacancies in the high schools for some time."

The doors didn't budge. So Josh joined another kind of army. A band of youth sports organizers who, little did they know, would ignite a generation.

Josh often called his 11-year-old brother outside their front door in the projects to watch the sun go down. He preached life philosophies and education and resilience. Imagine Bob's tolerance for such lectures. But they did share a hero. Jackie Robinson.

Josh Gibson teaches bunting techniques in May 1955.

On Oct. 15, 1946 — the same day the Cardinals beat the Indians in Game 7 of the World Series — Jackie's Negro League barnstorming team arrived in Omaha.

"The Little Negro, who has earned a tryout with the Brooklyn Dodgers, is acclaimed by at least one International League rival as the greatest bunter in baseball," The World-Herald wrote. Before the game, Robinson spoke at the Near North YMCA, encouraging black kids to pursue baseball while reminding them of the obstacles they had to overcome.

Exactly six months later, Jackie made his major-league debut with the Dodgers. Soon Josh went to work on a pitcher's mound behind Kellom.

Scoop. Dump. Pack.

He marked off a spot for home plate and from spring to fall, almost every night, Josh and Bob played catch. Sometimes for 10 minutes, sometimes for hours.

Pop. ... Pop.

Pop. ... Pop.

"It wasn't long before Robert could really hum that ball," Josh said.

Pop. ... Pop.

Pop. ... Pop.

There were times, Josh said, when Bob wanted to be off with the other boys, "but I kept him at it."

Big brother didn't stop with family. He assembled a team from the neighborhood. Rudy Skillman, Jerry Parks and Wendell Booth. Troy Richardson and Leon Chambers. Haskell Lee and Rodney Wead. They called each other by their mothers' first names, devoured day-old doughnuts from Petersen's Bakery and practiced at Burdette Field, where the diamond wasn't much smoother than the brick streets.

Josh timed base runners with his stopwatch. He launched fly balls halfway to Lake Street — two in the air at a time. He smashed grounders through the rocks, quizzing his infielders.

Runners on first and second, one out. Where do you go with the ball?

He mandated practice attendance, and, if Josh had to, he'd make home visits to pick up players. The only time he himself showed up late, he carried a stack of books from Creighton. Josh shared literature and theory with his most inquisitive players, but even when he finished his master's degree in '52 he couldn't get a teaching job.

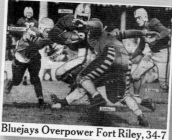

Bluejays Overpower Fort Riley, 34-7

Jackie & Joe at Creighton

Jackie Robinson actually visited Omaha once before his professional baseball days.

In 1942, Robinson had just been drafted into the Army and assigned to a segregated unit at Fort Riley, Kansas, alongside Joe Louis. Imagine America's two most prominent black athletes together in basic training in the middle of nowhere.

Robinson, a four-sport standout at UCLA before the war, joined the Fort Riley football team. But before the first game against the University of Missouri, he received a two-week leave. Why? Mizzou refused to play against a black player.

Robinson quit the team.

Three weeks later, Oct. 10, 1942, he and Louis traveled to Omaha with the renowned Army drill team. The 111-man detachment, comprising a 45-piece band, performed at halftime of the Creighton-Fort Riley football game.

There was no reference to Robinson in news accounts. But Louis made national news when he told a World-Herald reporter his boxing days were over.

"I'll be in my 30s after the war and that's too old," said Louis, 28, who, in fact, fought 15 more times between 1944 and '51.

That night, Robinson and Louis attended a party at the USO Center on 24th and Grant Streets before bunking at Fort Omaha.

As for the actual game, Fort Riley could've used Jackie. Creighton won 34-7, one of its last wins before it became a World War II casualty.

One month later, the Bluejays played their last-ever intercollegiate game.

He channeled his fury into the neighborhood. In August 1949, the Near North YMCA promoted Josh to physical director. His job description: Energize kids. Most had fathers, but they worked packinghouse jobs and came home late and tired.

"You got in trouble, Josh was like your daddy," Haskell Lee said. "He'd talk to ya."

He saved the hardest lessons for his little brother, whom he always called Robert. After practices, they stayed for more swings, more laps, more everything. One day little brother caught a bad hop and went running home with a cut above his eye. Their mother scolded Josh. *If he doesn't want to play, leave him alone.*

Robert always went back.

***

Fundamentals are fine, but what good is a baseball education without actual games?

Josh's junior high kids played a few white teams from Omaha, but the coach wasn't satisfied. He'd traveled halfway around the world. He needed to open his players' eyes wider. So he called little league coaches in small towns. Placed ads in The World-Herald with his phone number:

Games wanted!

He loaded the boys into a rental van or an Army truck with a canvas cover or Preston Love's orchestra bus, whatever he could find. Pulled out his Iowa map and drove them into the rural wilderness.

"Wooooo, just look at the corn."

Young Wendell Booth was so awed by the sight, his teammates nicknamed him "Corn."

The boys called themselves the Monarchs, just like the Negro League team in Kansas City. And they raised a lot of eyebrows when they rolled into towns like Hamburg, Onawa and Avoca.

In Woodbine on Aug. 20, 1948, the Monarchs marched in a 20-team town parade, then played the main event at the new Memorial Stadium before 2,000 people, helping raise $1,150 to fight the polio epidemic in Iowa's hardest-hit county.

The Y Monarchs midget baseball team.

The Monarchs usually won, but losses never sat right. "You gotta beat the ball to death," Josh told them, because you won't get the benefit of the doubt. In Griswold, the umpire was an old sheriff with a .45 in his holster. His chest protector was a baby mattress, and when the ball crossed home plate, he stammered, "Bbbbbb-steerike!"

When Josh didn't like a call, Wead said, he stormed his "big ass" out of the dugout as players held their collective breath.

"Josh raised hell in those white towns, man," Wead said. "We were so scared that those people would come out of the stands and jump on us. I imagine they didn't think blacks talked back."

Once Josh challenged the whole crowd to a brawl. Once he argued so persistently that the ump asked if he wanted to wear the mask. When he took it and squatted behind the plate, the ump threw him out.

Josh occasionally pulled the whole team off the field. He always brought them back.

In 1949, the year Jackie Robinson won MVP, the Monarchs traveled 1,850 miles. In '50, they played a game at Kansas City Blues Stadium, home of the real Monarchs. The road trip wasn't all grand. Hotels wouldn't accommodate them so they slept on pool tables at a Kansas City YMCA.

Eventually, Omaha's Near North Y bought a used charter bus for the team.

"We did more pushing than riding," Lee said. "We'd get caught on those old country roads at night and we'd wait until somebody would stop and give a jump."

In August 1950, they made it all the way to Wayne, Nebraska, for the state midget tournament. No team from the Near North Side had ever qualified. Bus troubles cut short the Monarchs' warmup, but they edged Alliance, 5-2.

Softball in Omaha

Three months after Joe Louis whacked Max Schmeling at Yankee Stadium, the heavyweight champion whiffed in Omaha.

Louis' barnstorming softball team, the "Brown Bombers," faced Nebraska's state champions at Falstaff Park in September 1938. Louis committed two errors at first base and struck out three times at the plate, but his team rallied to a 4-2 win and drew 2,800 fans.

This was no celebrity novelty act.

During the FDR era, fast-pitch softball — not baseball — was Omaha's favorite recreational sport. Newspaper tycoon William Randolph Hearst started a national tournament in the early 1930s, invested $1,000 in a trophy and ordered his Omaha Bee-News to start a league.

Initially, only the first baseman and the catcher wore gloves, and the mound was closer to home plate. But the game quickly exploded. Falstaff Park, at 24th and Vinton Streets, hosted the biggest games. As many as 3,500 fans paid a quarter to watch on weekends.

By '44, Omaha had more than 200 men's softball teams, including several on the Near North Side.

Phenom pitcher Clarence "Ace" Hill pitched for a state champion at 16 years old and toured the country as a hired gun in '47. His "windmill" arm motion intimidated batters.

"I threw that thing 100 miles an hour," Hill said decades later. "I had a change-up, a riser, a drop. I threw it between my legs, behind my back."

Bob Gibson might have been the next Ace Hill if Jackie Robinson hadn't come along. Before he dazzled overhand, Gibson dominated underhand for Kellom in the school league.

"We just kicked ass," Rodney Wead said. "Nobody could hit Gibson's softball."

Next up: Blair. Bob, too wild to pitch often, gave up just one hit and the Monarchs stole 13 bases in a 10-7 win.

In the championship against Oakdale, Bob doubled home two runs in the first inning. That was the difference in a 4-2 win.

"Who would believe some guys from the projects would take the whole state?" Wead said.

***

In hindsight, it makes total sense, right? How wouldn't they win? *They had Bob Gibson.*

Omaha Star, Nov. 3, 1950:

—William White Photo

"Y" Monarch Victory Dinner

Pictured is the gay crowd at the Y-Monarchs' second annual victory dinner at Jerry's and Johnny's Drive-In, 3210 No. 30th St. The Monarchs, who are the midget baseball team of the Near Northside YMCA and their guests were honored by Mr. and Mrs. Gerald Morris of the Crosstown Cleaners and Mr. John Burton of Jerry's and Johnny's Drive-In— with a marvelous chicken dinner. The Monarchs, the 1950 Nebraska Midget Baseball Champions heard a speech by Mr. John R. Butler, executive secretary of the Near North Side YMCA in which they were pointed out the role they must play as true champions of our community; the Monarchs were also cited by their manager and coach, "Josh" Gibson for the fine "never say die" spirit and cooperation exhibited during the past baseball season. Each member of the team received a championship emblem a certificate of merit from the American Legion and a championship indentification card. The Y-Monarchs' special guests included: Mr. Ralph Adams, the master of ceremonies, Mr. Gerald Morris, Mr. Benny McPhaulls, Mr. John E. Douthy, and Mr. John Favors who led the group in enthusiastic innings of cheer and song.

But the Monarchs grew up in a 2-square-mile box hearing stories that blacks couldn't fly because their brains were too small. Their parents couldn't work in downtown offices. Their mentor couldn't teach in high schools. You hear *can't* so many times that you internalize your inferiority, Love Jr. said.

"There must be something wrong with me."

To believe they could succeed, the Monarchs first had to *see* it. Then they really took off.

"To experience being announced 'Rodney Wead, number so-and-so, now come to bat,' to be identified as truly a human being, to hear the applause of the crowd was truly remarkable. I think that is the reason I am who I am now, because of those trips that Josh put together."

Wead, a history professor, knows this story better than anyone. His grandfather was murdered by white men in Arkansas in 1919. His family fled north to Omaha, where his dad changed his last name — Weed to Wead — and worked at Swift packinghouse with Malcolm X's father. Rodney grew up with the Gibsons, shadowed Satchel Paige and Duke Ellington, chauffeured Martin Luther King Jr. and protested George Wallace — all in North Omaha.

Seventy-one years after the Monarchs' first practice, Wead returned from St. Louis — where he lives now — because Omaha named a street after him. An hour before the ceremony, he shared an IHOP booth with Haskell Lee. They're Bob Gibson's only surviving Monarch teammates.

Their weathered hands shredded pancakes as they shared flashes of childhood. The way shortstop Woody Grant held his hat every time he jumped for a ball. The way second baseman Isaiah "Zeke" Davis threw 100-mph rockets to first base. Sometimes it hit the glove, Lee said. "Sometimes it would be in the bleachers."

Davis eventually got his engineering degree and worked on space shuttles at Cape Canaveral. He didn't cave when Wead pestered him for state secrets.

"I would say, 'Dav, what's a ballistic missile?' He'd say, 'I really can't.' And I said, 'Get out of here! I'm not gonna tell.' He helped design the first nose cone after Sputnik went up. I just did a eulogy for him. He died just a month ago, Hoss."

"Zeke did? Oh man, I didn't know that."

Gibson couldn't join them at IHOP. He was in St. Louis reuniting with the 1968 National League champions. Probably sitting at a diner just like this telling stories with Lou Brock and Tim McCarver. Seventeen strikeouts! But Gibby's oldest teammates know the truth: He wouldn't be a Cardinal if he weren't first a Monarch.

In 1950, they celebrated their midget championship with a victory chicken dinner at Jerry's and Johnny's Drive-In on North 30th Street. Josh praised the Monarchs' unity and "never-say-die" spirit. Then he and his little brother went back to work.

Pop. … Pop.

Pop. … Pop.

Over the next year, 1951, war raged in Korea. "I Love Lucy" debuted on CBS. Willie Mays won Rookie of the Year.

Meanwhile, the Sayers brothers migrated from Kansas to the Near North Side. Marlin Briscoe moved from California to the South Omaha projects. Johnny Rodgers arrived as a baby in the River Bottoms.

Pop. … Pop.

Pop. … Pop.

Loud enough for most of the neighborhood to hear, including a skinny kid from Alabama who'd fallen in love with a different ball.

Bob Boozer was about to get his first lesson in rebounding.

Bob Gibson in 1953.

Chapter 2

Raising Roofs

THE HOUSE STANDS ALONE beneath a towering catalpa tree, one block from North Omaha's main artery.

Plywood boards shutter the front door and windows. Gray paint peels from wood siding. Next to an empty Corona bottle, a crack in the foundation zigzags like a lightning bolt. Three skinny white pillars hold up the porch, where a crossword puzzle book squeezes into a small black mailbox and a year-old Sports Illustrated shrivels on the floor.

Inside, there's 900 square feet on the main floor and another half story above. Bedrooms, a living room and a kitchen. Memories of a mother and father combing through report cards and distributing allowances in coins. But no way to see in. The white homes that once stood on this street — tight as teeth — have all been pulled. Demolished. For some reason, the bulldozer spared the 114-year-old shell at 2402 N. 25th St.

Picture its prime, when a gangly teenager burst out the front door, down those four porch steps and bounced his basketball toward the pulse of 24th Street.

Bob Boozer's childhood home near 25th and Erskine Streets still stands today, the only building on a block once full of life.

Bob Boozer, by family rule, had to return to the porch when the streetlights flickered on. That left plenty of time to play at his home away from home: the Near North YMCA.

Boozer covered those four blocks hundreds, if not thousands, of times, starting in the late 1940s when the Y was in the old Webster Telephone Exchange Building, 2213 Lake St. He and his friends wore out the concrete floors. All day Saturday, after school on weekdays, even during the Lake School lunch hour. They scarfed day-old rolls,

The Near North YMCA, housed in the 1940s in the Webster Telephone Exchange Building, was Bob Boozer's second home.

chugged from milk cartons and played shirts and skins, returning to class smelly but satisfied.

The hoops weren't quite 10 feet. That's because they were in the basement.

"You had to shoot a line drive shot if you didn't want to hit the ceiling," Boozer said in an interview before he died in 2012.

Boozer always had a jumper, but he lacked strength. In high school, he tried out for a distinguished neighborhood team — the Y Travelers — loaded with grown men and high school standouts, including acrobatic point guard Bob Gibson. Bob's big brother Josh ran the show.

Boozer had never met Josh Gibson until tryout day. His first impression was Josh's substantial rear end.

"He was showing me how to box out. And he put his butt into me and rooted me out from underneath the basket. He rooted me to half court. And that's when I first learned how to get a rebound."

Boozer would carry the lesson the rest of his career, to Wilt's cathedral, the Olympic medal stand and the Champagne-soaked NBA champions' locker room. But rooting out the enemies of Boozer's neighborhood wasn't so simple.

Bob Boozer in 1954.

Playland Park in Council Bluffs, pictured here in 1959, was one of the few entertainment places in the Omaha area where blacks were allowed.

As the 1940s ended, North Omaha didn't feel any less segregated than Alabama, where Boozer was born. When a black man tried to order burgers in South Omaha, he was charged extra before noticing a sign: "No colored trade solicited." One night, four young women — two black, two white — attended a downtown exhibit honoring America's fight for liberty. But afterward, a downtown restaurant refused to serve them.

"You wouldn't think of being in the Benson area after dark," said Rodney Wead, Boozer's friend and peer. "You'd get your butt beat and run out of there quick by the police or the residents."

Crosstown Roller Rink denied admission to blacks, except on Wednesday nights. Peony Park prohibited blacks entirely. That left Playland Park in Council Bluffs, where Boozer saw a black man atop a dunk tank, next to a sign: "Dump the n-----."

Eighty percent of blacks didn't graduate high school, partly because they were barred from jobs outside service or manual labor. Why put in extra work for white-collar jobs that weren't there? Corporations like Union Pacific and Coca-Cola didn't hire blacks. Neither did streetcar companies, laundromats or ice cream parlors.

Sacred Heart Catholic Church at 22nd and Binney Streets, near the heart of North Omaha, refused to accept black parishioners. An Omaha doctor refused to treat a 4-year-old black girl. The downtown YMCA allowed Boozer and blacks to swim in the pool, but drained the water once they left. You're never going there again, his mother told him.

Each incident, Boozer said, looking back over seven decades, felt like an object hitting you on the shoulder. It always bounces off, but it leaves something buried inside.

"You remember that stuff."

Like most of his neighbors, Boozer's first memories were of the Jim Crow South.

His dad tended the coal-fired boilers at the University of Alabama. One night, after bosses passed him over for another promotion, John Boozer came home and told his family to pack up.

"We're going north."

While American soldiers headed overseas to fight Hitler and Japan, the Boozers joined the second Great Migration. Bob was just starting school when he boarded a train from Tuscaloosa to Memphis, then to St. Louis, then Kansas City, and finally Omaha's Union Station. He was led to North 24th Street, just off Binney. His family dropped its belongings and moved onto the third floor of a cousin's house.

Dad went to work loading cow hides onto trains at Armour packinghouse. Mom got a maid job at a downtown hotel. Soon they bought the house — 1½ stories with a gabled roof — on North 25th Street.

From 1940 to '50, Omaha's black population nearly doubled — from 12,000 to about 22,000. Newcomers jammed into little white houses, sleeping on relatives' couches or floors, as black leaders like Woodrow Morgan tried to push the neighborhood walls.

Morgan was a Tuskegee Airman flying an armed reconnaissance mission over Rome on May 26, 1944 — 11 days before the Normandy invasion — when his plane went down behind enemy lines. He spent the next year in one of Mussolini's prison camps before coming home to North Omaha a hero. Morgan bought a house at 31st and Parker Streets, just west of the black box. His new white neighbors hurled insults into his phone and rocks through his windows. The veteran stuck it out, but resistance persisted.

In prestigious Kountze Place, just north of the boundary, white residents received penny postcards reminding them of the dangers of a "Negro invasion."

If you want to stop communism in the U.S.A., see that restrictive covenants are enforced!

The U.S. Supreme Court had ruled that neighborhood contracts preventing sales to blacks were unconstitutional. But enforcement was lax and ideologies entrenched.

A World-Herald reader wrote this in the Public Pulse on March 27, 1948:

> *"While it is undoubtedly true that a colored person cannot patronize certain hotels and bars and cafes that cater exclusively to white folks, just what is there to prevent the more well-to-do among the colored folks building their own hotels, cafes, etc.? … The colored person complains because he must (?) live among his own color. Just what does this mean? Are they shamed of their fellow Negroes? Just why do they moan and groan incessantly because they cannot live among white folks?"*

Blacks may have avoided the trouble if Near North Side houses weren't so dilapidated. Excluding the housing projects, fewer than 20 new homes had been built in the neighborhood since World War I. Half of black homes needed repairs or condemnation. The chairman of the Douglas County Board, Roman Hruska, described black housing as "abominable."

DePorres Club

Omaha Street Railway Co. Cries For Drivers --- Negroes Ask
For A Chance --- BUT . . .
THE STREET RAILWAY CO. REFUSES TO HIRE NEGRO DRIVERS.
Let's Help Make Equal Opportunity Real. Help Make Democracy
Work in Omaha and Resist the Vicious Evil of Communism.
——ATTEND AND INFORM YOUR FRIENDS——
PUBLIC   MEETING
FOR SOME NEGRO DRIVERS ON OMAHA'S BUSES
ZION BAPTIST CHURCH, 2215 Grant St.
FRIDAY, DECEMBER 14th -- 8 P. M.
—— SPONSORED BY OMAHA DePORRES CLUB ——

Twelve years before black college students staged the famous sit-in at Woolworth's lunch counter in North Carolina, the De-Porres Club did the same at an Omaha restaurant.

Four years before Martin Luther King Jr. led the famous bus boycott in Alabama, the DePorres Club did the same to Omaha streetcars and buses.

Creighton University was a long way from the Deep South, but the Rev. John Markoe recognized sin when he saw it. So in November 1947, he organized one of America's earliest civil rights groups.

This unusual mix of white college kids and North Omaha blacks confronted segregation and discrimination in bold, relentless methods. In 1948, 30 members staged a sit-in at a Douglas County Courthouse diner that refused to serve blacks.

Markoe, a former All-American football player and West Point grad, didn't shy from controversy. One of his group's first initiatives was pushing nearby Catholic churches to allow black students in their schools. That prompted Creighton's president to push the DePorres Club off campus.

Markoe's group, named after a Peruvian monk, eventually began meeting at the Omaha Star on North 24th Street, where it found a home and a focus: discrimination in the workforce.

The DePorres Club and Mildred Brown's Omaha Star led boycotts of the local Coca-Cola Bottling Co. and Reed's Ice Cream, successfully coaxing their owners to hire blacks. Protests didn't always follow that script, though.

In July 1950, the DePorres Club and the Omaha Star called out Edholm-Sherman Laundry — a Near North business whose clientele was 70 percent black — for refusing to hire blacks as clerks. A boycott pressured Mrs. Edholm, but she never gave in. Six months later, she went out of business.

The DePorres Club didn't fight battles alone. It found allies with local branches of the NAACP and Urban League. Up-and-coming civil rights leader Whitney Young headed the Omaha Urban League. If a business didn't hire blacks, Young might play the role of diplomat, warning the business owner of the DePorres Club's intention to picket or boycott.

The toughest fight came against the city's street-car and bus company, which refused to hire black drivers. In 1951, activists posted pickets and distributed handbills.

"Negro GIs Drive Tanks, Jeeps and Trucks. Why Not Buses and Street Cars in Omaha?"

Three years later, the DePorres Club finally claimed victory. Omaha hired its first black drivers.

The DePorres Club remained a force through October 1954, inspiring a brand of activism that made North Omaha a civil rights leader in the '60s.

DePorres Club members, including Rodney Wead's father (front left), protest Reed's Ice Cream in 1953 for not hiring blacks.

"Most Caucasians," said the future U.S. senator, "are not bigots or malicious but only bewildered and misinformed bystanders ... overwhelmingly possessed with inertia and are likely to be governed by tradition rather than by conviction."

Soon, Omaha built three more housing projects — 700 units — in addition to Logan Fontenelle. While the neighborhood scrambled for beds, the Boozers entrenched at 25th and Erskine. That's where Bob collected comic books, which he traded with his friend up the street, Ernie Chambers. You had to give three basic comics to get a classic like "Frankenstein." Damage your cover and you're paying extra.

"It was almost like a little barter system," Chambers said.

Boozer didn't pay a dime to see his real heroes. When the Negro League buses turned onto Erskine Street and stopped in front of Patton's boardinghouse, the driver hit the air horn. "And I would hit the door," Boozer said.

He flew off his porch, sprinted across the street and blurted to the first man off the bus: "Can I be batboy?"

Major cities anchored the Negro Leagues, but in order to gain fans and revenue, they barnstormed, challenging local semi-pro teams. Boozer rode the buses to Rosenblatt Stadium and Council Bluffs' Legion Park. He shagged bats and helmets for the Kansas City Monarchs, the Birmingham Black Barons and, best of all, the Indianapolis Clowns with Satchel Paige.

During the seventh inning, the Clowns spiced up the game with an act of shadow ball. Their slugger would crush an imaginary ball back, back, back. He rounded the bases as the outfielders gave chase. Then just before he touched home plate, the catcher — out of nowhere — placed the tag on him.

"The people in the stands got a big kick out of that," Boozer said.

***

Thanksgiving Day 1949.

In snowy Detroit, the Bears hammered the Lions, 24-7. In South Bend, No. 1 Notre Dame prepared to smack USC, 32-0. In North Omaha, residents gathered on a windy, 40-degree afternoon for their own turkey tradition.

The annual Coal Bowl at Burdette Field matched the neighborhood's finest black football players, from teenagers to grown men. It was tackle. It was vicious. It was freedom.

Josh Gibson coached his YMCA Monarchs at Burdette in the summer. But come Thanksgiving, he usually played quarterback. The '49 Coal Bowl was tough on quarterbacks. Central High's Bobby Fairchild thrice led the "Pirates" inside the "All-Stars' " 5-yard line. "But each time the All-Star defense became as formidable as a fourth helping of turkey and mashed potatoes," according to The World-Herald report.

With three minutes left, one of the five Gibson brothers, Fred, nearly broke the scoreless tie when he intercepted a Pirate pass and returned it 80 yards for a touchdown. But a holding penalty wiped it out. Oh, the controversy.

Very few black athletes in the 1940s and early '50s competed for high schools or colleges. What satisfied their competitive hunger? What kept them sane amid discrimination?
The most fanatical rec league culture you can imagine.

There was boxing, badminton, tumbling, wrestling, volleyball, golf, tennis, girls basketball, mostly organized by the Near North YMCA. Eugene Skinner, the first black principal in Omaha Public Schools, hung up his suit and tie on weekends and led the Near North soccer team to back-to-back city championships.

There were table tennis tournaments and fishing expeditions, ceramics and woodworking classes, tap dance recitals and talent shows, even wheelchair basketball. And who was behind most of it? Josh Gibson.

Josh Gibson

If OPS wasn't going to hire him to teach and coach, he was going to turn North Omaha into one monster P.E. class.

The most serious team of all was men's basketball. The Y Travelers were older than Josh's youth baseball team — late teens and 20s — but they also toured the Midwest. They were the first black team to compete in Omaha's best league. And in 1954, Josh led them to the city championship.

Bob Gibson shined at Creighton from 1954-57.

Bob Rose, a former Omaha University standout, started at guard. But the real star was Bob Gibson, a "jumping-jack trick shot artist," according to the Omaha Star. He grew up shooting line drives in the Y basement, too.

Gibson had started ninth grade south of 5 foot and 100 pounds. So small that Tech's freshman football coach, Neal Mosser, shooed him away.
But by his senior year, Gibson was a 6-foot, 165-pound all-city basketball guard. That spring, he earned all-city in baseball, too, earning a contract offer from the renowned Kansas City Monarchs.

Go to college, Josh ordered.

Bob wanted to play basketball at Indiana, but he settled for the school half a mile away, Creighton. For a while, nobody in the city could match him. Then his old friend from the YMCA basement hit a growth spurt.

At dinner time, Viola Boozer made sure no chair sat empty. Every night, Boozer's mom walked in the door, crashed on the bed for a few minutes, rose and cooked dinner, demanding that her family eat together.

Dad had a seventh-grade education. Mom made it to ninth. But they scrutinized every report card, making clear that Bob and older sister Mary would go to college. One problem: They had money only for Mary.

In high school, the Boozers allotted their kids 50 cents a day for lunch and transportation. A streetcar ride cost a dime. If you rode one way, you got a 40-cent lunch. If you rode both ways, you got a 30-cent lunch.

"So we walked to school every day," Boozer said. "In the winter, you name it. We were walking."

Mary hiked 2 miles downtown, joining Rodney Wead and 35 blacks in Omaha Central's class of 1953. Bob took a shorter route, a mile and a half, following Bob Gibson to the superior basketball school.

Technical High.

A product of the post-World War I boom, Tech opened in 1923 with OPS officials claiming it was the largest school west of Chicago. Original plans called for just 1,200 students, but demand was so high that architects started over. Why? Tech specialized in trades.

The theory was simple: American factories would follow the educated labor. So if Omaha trained the next generation of mechanics, electricians, welders, carpenters and plumbers, the local economy would thrive.

Enrollment at Tech High peaked in 1940 at about 3,700 students.

It wasn't all grunt work. Tech students fixed Model Ts. They studied aeronautics. Some hosted radio shows in a state-of-the-art broadcasting studio. In 1940, just after Josh Gibson graduated, enrollment peaked at about 3,700 students. Central High couldn't hold that many. Neither could South nor North. But Tech, constructed for $3.5 million (more than $50 million in today's money), rose five stories and stretched three blocks along Cuming Street. It featured the finest amenities: two gymnasiums, a swimming pool, a 2,200-seat auditorium, marble staircases, secret tunnels, a greenhouse and an underground stream.

Tech High specialized in teaching trades.

From the beginning, Tech was a melting pot of rich kids, poor kids, immigrants, natives, Russians, Italians, Jews, you name it. But following the second Great Migration, most of its best athletes were black.

Boozer was no prodigy. He played junior varsity as a 5-foot-11 10th-grader. He loved the game, but he also liked to sneak out and ride around in John Ewing's '39 Chevy. Friends called him Baby Boozer.

Then the summer before 11th grade, 1953, he shot up.

Six-foot-1 ...

Boozer's strides off the porch got a little longer, his drive a lot stronger. He was growing so fast he couldn't walk and talk at the same time. So he started jumping rope. His buddies led him through agility drills. He went one-on-one with Johnny Nared, who went on to be an all-city guard at Central.

Six-foot-3 ...

Suddenly Boozer had visions of attending college without Mom and Dad's help. Charles Bryant, a standout football player, had gone from North Omaha to all-conference honors at Nebraska. Gibson was on scholarship at Creighton. Why not him, too?

Bob Boozer with Tech High coach Neal Mosser in 1954.

Maggie King

She grew up in the same Logan Fontenelle projects unit as Bob Gibson — 2212 Charles St. She walked the Tech High hallways with Bob Boozer.

Maggie King nearly beat them both to the national stage. While Gibby and Booz overcame racial injustice to be great, the magnificent Maggie confronted gender barriers, too.

High schools offered girls only one sport in the '50s — tennis. But Josh Gibson's programs gave Maggie more chances to compete. She shined in basketball, softball, volleyball, running, tennis, table tennis and box hockey. One event made her extraordinary: the high jump.

In July 1954, King leaped 5-foot-2 at a city parks and recreation meet, the second-best women's mark in the country that year — 1¾ inches better than gold at the national AAU meet.

Remember, this predated Dick Fosbury's backward flop. In the '50s, high jumpers curled over the bar, stomach down. Maggie cleared the bar like a hurdler.

Maggie's single mother raised nine kids. Older brother Tony excelled in boxing. Younger brother Bill shined in basketball. But Maggie became a phenom, attracting praise from famous black athletes Jesse Owens and Toni Stone.

In '55, the Crosstown Athletic Club, a black organization, funded King's Pan-Am Games tryout in Chicago. She suffered an injury on her second jump and settled for third place — 4-foot-10.

Maggie's athleticism captivated her believers, but she lacked expertise and opportunity. Word spread that she didn't have the coaching or funds to pursue the '56 Games in Melbourne. The U.S. Olympic committee wasn't happy.

"You proved at the Pan-American tryouts that you were real Olympic material," said Roxanne Andersen, U.S. women's track and field chairman. "It seems incredible that the city of Omaha would not get behind a prospective Olympian."

In March '56, pole vaulter Bob Richards came to Omaha and King detailed her unorthodox style.

She fascinated the Olympic gold medalist, who called for a pencil and paper. Twenty minutes later, Richards handed Maggie a set of sketches and instructions on the "roll" technique.

"If you can jump 5-2 now, perfection of this style should enable you to go 5-8 or 5-9 and break the world's record."

As he left, Richards urged Maggie to train diligently: "See you in Melbourne."

From that point, North Omaha rallied behind the quiet King. Local businesses, schools and coaches contributed time and money. Maggie set a personal-best in practice, 5-3, half an inch higher than the IOC's qualifying height.

But she felt the pressure. During a softball game in August, King fainted and spent the night in the hospital. The doctor diagnosed exhaustion.

One week later, Maggie and her mom boarded a plane for the first time and flew to Washington, D.C., for the Olympic tryouts. She cleared 4-11, fourth-best in the country. Not high enough.

King returned to Tech High and graduated in '57. She turned down a scholarship to Tennessee A&I, but in September '58 she joined the Army instead.

Maggie spent the next 23 years traveling the world as an eye, ear, nose and throat specialist before retiring in Texas. She died Valentine's Day 2014.

Sixty-five years after Maggie's stunning jump at the city track meet, few remember her talent. But if she came around today, it's hard not to wonder: How high could she go?

Six-foot-5 ...

As a junior, he averaged 19.7 points per game and made all-city. Boozer could catch the ball just off the block, fake one way, turn the other and make jumper after jumper. When he wanted a challenge, Bob practiced with his eyes closed.

He grew another inch before 12th grade. John Butler, the Y director, gave Boozer a key, so he could train at night. The Near North YMCA had constructed a new building at 22nd and Grant and the rims were finally 10 feet.

Boozer's dunks proved they were sturdy.

***

The heroes always returned. Joe Louis. Jackie Robinson. Hank Aaron. They all made public appearances on the Near North Side in the mid-'50s. The most eloquent arrived in the final days of Omaha's 100th anniversary year, 1954.

Jesse Owens

Jesse Owens, who defied Hitler at the 1936 Olympics, headlined Tech High's third annual all-sports show. It was the Near North Y where he delivered a life message tailor-made for a 17-year-old basketball prospect.

"When you go to college," Owens told the crowd, "the athletic department will put a pair of imaginary rose-colored glasses on you. When you depart the campus, the same athletic department will take the glasses off of you. For the first time in four years, you will see the world as it really is."

Companies will hire you because of your accomplishments, Owens said. But when you stop making headlines, they'll see no value in you. They'll cut you loose. You'll wander from job to job and become a "bum."

"Go to school to get an education. Then when the medals you have won are tarnished and the banners given you have gathered so much dust that you can't read the year 1954, the wisdom and knowledge that you have acquired will be the championship that will be the dearest and most valuable to you."

Boozer knew he couldn't get the education without a scholarship. And basketball was his ticket. He broke city scoring records that winter. He averaged 25.7 points per game and led Tech High to a 15-2 record. He played the game, according to a 1955 World-Herald story, "as if he invented it."

But state basketball championships eluded the Trojans. In 1952, foul trouble doomed them against Fremont — Gibson blamed the refs. Coach Neal Mosser, who started four black players, always told the Trojans to leave no doubt. If you let them stay around so the referees can have an opportunity to take it away from you, they will.

Two years later, Tech met Scottsbluff in the state semifinals at the NU Coliseum. Boozer had 19 points, but he couldn't get free in the second half as Scottsbluff grabbed the lead. When the clock hit zeroes, the tallest man on the floor broke down like a child.

"I literally stood in the middle of the floor and just cried."

Two weeks later, he was back at the Y, exchanging passes with Creighton's Bob Gibson as they led Josh's Travelers over the Minneapolis Wizards, 91-47.

The following Sunday morning, Boozer made The World-Herald's all-state team, joining a skinny redhead from Hastings whom columnist Gregg McBride called a "smooth manipulator and strategist." Tom Osborne opted to stay in Hastings for college. Boozer wanted to get out of Omaha. Preferably to Iowa.

Mosser sent the Hawkeyes coach a letter of interest. When he got a response, he called Boozer from study hall and sat him down.

I want you to see something, Mosser said. Brace yourself, this is the way life is gonna be.

Boozer read the letter, which echoed the letter Bob Gibson received from his dream school, Indiana, two years earlier.

We've met our quota of black players.

That spring day in 1955, Boozer returned to the little house on 25th Street shouldering a familiar twinge. The same sense of anger his father felt a decade earlier, when he came home from shoveling coal into the flames and decided to move his family north.

In June, Bob graduated from Tech and found a fallback plan for college. Kansas State. The future All-American, Olympian and NBA champ packed his bags, stepped off his porch and headed south alone.

He had all the fire he needed.

Deacon Jones

Charles "Deacon" Jones didn't have an address in North Omaha. But the two-time Olympian always had a dinner plate.

Jones was 13 when he left a troubled home in St. Paul, Minnesota, for Father Flanagan's Boys Town, west of Omaha. Where did a black kid far from home find friends? Eleven miles east, in the heart of the black neighborhood — the Logan Fontenelle projects.

On weekends, Jones hung out with Bob Gibson and Rodney Wead, regularly eating meals at Wead's.

Back at Boys Town, Jones was an all-state halfback in football and an all-state guard on the Cowboys' state championship basketball team and right fielder on the state championship baseball team. Pretty impressive considering Boys Town, unlike today, competed against the state's largest schools.

But distance running really set Jones apart.

"He was like a high-powered, eight-cylinder Cadillac that could run all day at 60 mph," said George Pfeifer, who coached Jones at Boys Town.

In 1954, Jones broke the national high school record in the mile with a time of 4 minutes, 17.6 seconds. At Iowa, he won an NCAA cross country championship and a track national title in the two-mile run.

Jones broke the American record in the steeplechase in 1957 and finished top-10 in the Olympics in '56 and '60.

"I was definitely a rarity in those days," Jones said before his death in 2007. "I was a black athlete from Nebraska who was a distance runner. People kind of did a double take when they saw me out there."

Chapter 3

Packinghouse Pride

ALARM CLOCKS BUZZED in the dark.

The men of the Near North Side put on their denim overalls, sipped their coffee and skimmed their newspapers — What did Ike say yesterday? They walked to North 24th Street and handed jitney drivers a quarter, sliding into black cars with long bench seats.

Squeeze together now.

Through the chute of sleepy buildings and over the brick street, they rolled south like a funeral procession. Past Carter's Cafe and Skeet's BBQ and the Fair Deal Cafe — all brand-new. Past Creighton University and Joslyn Art Museum as the sky brightened over downtown.

Follow the stench.

In 1955, roughly half of all black workers made this morning commute to South Omaha. Most businesses wouldn't hire them, but muscle and grit mattered more than race in the city's dominant industry.

Meatpacking.

Blacks shared the packinghouse floors with whites, working as drivers, penners, shacklers, stickers, hoisters, skinners, rumpers, gutters, splitters, butchers, boners, trimmers, dippers, luggers.

The stockyards in 1953 with South Omaha in the background.

Bob Boozer's dad clocked in at Armour. Bob Gibson's oldest brother worked at Swift. Gale Sayers' dad worked at Cudahy. So did Johnny Rodgers' grandpa.

Meatpacking lured black families to Omaha, put food on their tables and established a work ethic that toughened sons and daughters. Motivated them, too.

"A lot of us who grew up in that environment, we wanted to do better than our parents," said Lew Garrison, a 1964 Tech High grad who played quarterback at Omaha University. "We didn't want the kind of jobs they wanted."

Thousands of livestock pens surround the Livestock Exchange Building in 1947.

The jitney carpools rolled 6 miles down 24th Street, then turned right on Q Street, crossing the viaduct and, with the sun rising behind them — behold! — America's butcher shop.

Thousands of livestock pens spread through the valley as far west as they could see. On L Street, trucks backed up for 3 miles waiting to turn onto Buckingham Avenue, where they unloaded cattle, hogs and sheep into the market. Commission agents assigned them pens and buyers examined the stock from elevated walkways, securing deals with a handshake.

Looming over the proceedings stood the magnificent 11-story Livestock Exchange Building with its Italian Renaissance architecture. Curious observers — even tourists — could witness the whole experience. Except the dirtiest work.

The Union Stockyards was such a sight that tourists could view the animals waiting to be butchered.

That happened behind closed doors in 19 slaughterhouses. Purchased cattle were driven up ramps to the top level — the kill floor — where they filed into a narrow stall. A "knocker" with a sledgehammer stood over the animal and swung for the forehead. When the beast dropped unconscious, a shackler wrapped a chain around the cow's hind legs, flipping 1,000 pounds upside down. A third man slit the cow's throat before a fourth worker cut off its head.

Over and over and over. The line never stopped moving.

Every day, $2 million changed hands. Six million gallons of water flowed through the Stockyards. The annual profits from manure alone matched the Florida citrus crop.

If all the animals in 1955 had lined up — one per 10 feet — they would have wrapped 13,000 miles. Halfway around the world. At one plant alone, 2,500 workers slaughtered almost 10,000 animals per day, one every three seconds.

Haskell Lee once swore he'd never do the work. But like thousands of blacks before him, Lee — Bob Gibson's old teammate from the YMCA Monarchs — determined that killing cows was his best way to make a living. He was 18. One day during his break, he visited the kill floor where Red Walker — "Big Red" — handed him the sledgehammer. *You want to try?* Lee missed his spot and the angry bull escaped the stall.

"Man," Lee said, "you should've seen guys running."

On Dec. 1, 1955, a 42-year-old black seamstress boarded a Montgomery, Alabama, bus and sat down in the "colored" section. Rosa Parks did not intend to cause a stir. But moments later, the white section filled and the driver ordered her to give up her seat to a white man. She refused, prompting her arrest, the beginning of a yearlong bus boycott and the unofficial birth of the civil rights movement.

Farmers across Nebraska and Iowa often lined up for hours to sell to the highest bidder.

Later that week, Omaha's Union Stockyards celebrated a milestone, too, overtaking Chicago for yearly receipts with 6,764,140 animals. The signs went up:

"World's Largest Livestock Market and Meat Packing Center."

It only took 70 years, hundreds of thousands of immigrants and millions of gallons of whiskey. Don't get tipsy now. Understanding the economic link between North and South Omaha demands a sober mind and a short history lesson.

Back in the 1860s, about the time Nebraska earned statehood, cowboys tried to move beef to Eastern cities. The problem? The railroads were nowhere near their Texas herds. Cattle drives made folk heroes, but they didn't make much sense. Rather than walking longhorns north to Kansas railheads to sell, William Paxton found an alternative. He stocked the Great Plains, starting a cattle ranch near Ogallala, Nebraska. Proximity to the Union Pacific Railroad made life easier, but there was another benefit: Texas longhorns were lean and stringy. Up north, cattle could put on more fat.

Beef production boomed following the Civil War. So did the Chicago stockyards, where western producers delivered to eastern buyers with help from innovative refrigerated boxcars.

But wait a minute. Pull out a map. There were 800 miles between Ogallala and Chicago. Why not split the difference? Start a market closer to the beef supply with access to a major railroad and river.

A Wyoming cattle baron named Alexander Swan made it happen. He partnered with six Omaha businessmen, including Paxton and John Creighton. They bought 2,000 acres south of the city at $1.67 an acre. They set aside 200 for the stockyards and committed the other 1,800 to building a town.

William Paxton

On Dec. 1, 1883, the Union Stockyards of Omaha was born. The first headquarters was the Drexel family farmhouse, where they stored money in the kitchen pantry and served booze in the basement.

In 1885, the first slaughterhouse sprouted. Hotels, saloons and brothels quickly followed. The timid and meek had no place here. In the early years, a mayor was mysteriously found dead with a bullet in his head. Edward Cudahy Jr. was abducted before his father, the richest man in town, paid the $25,000 ransom — the cops finally caught his captors. Sir Thomas Lipton, a Scottish tea merchant, built the third packinghouse. When he visited, he was stunned to find so many pistols in the cloakroom. Reminded him of an armory.

South Omaha didn't need guns to have a good time. Immigrants slugged it out in muddy streets. Cowboys fought bulls in an 8,000-seat amphitheater. Within the Stockyards, wooden drain plugs from the water troughs became a popular weapon — "Whoever had the biggest plug or the biggest fist got his cattle weighed first," one said.

Amid all the violence, integrity never lost its currency. Livestock sales happened so fast — sealed with a handshake, of course — that any whiff of dishonesty kicked dirt on a man's reputation. People didn't deal with scoundrels.

Swan wanted to call his creation "New Edinburgh," but like Lipton, he didn't have the stomach to stick around. So Paxton became the face of the Stockyards, which by 1890 — just six years after the first herd — had risen to third nationally in livestock sales, including 1.7 million cattle.

Officially, it became South Omaha. But a reporter christened the place with a nickname.

The Magic City.

The Magic City, officially known as South Omaha, bustled with activity. This scene looks north from 24th and N Streets in 1914.

***

As William Paxton and Alexander Swan dreamed of wealth, the ancestors of pro football's first black quarterback dreamed of liberty. And Marlin Briscoe's family didn't let dreams slip away.

Down in Tennessee, the Civil War set his great-grandfather free, but Govner Moore waited for more. He was scheduled to receive land and money once his former slaveowner died. The plan fell apart. Coming home from school one day, Govner's children quarreled with kids they weren't supposed to quarrel with. Hours later, vigilante white men came to their door. Marlin Briscoe's great-grandmother grabbed her gun and stood her ground.

"The Ku Klux Klan or Night Riders or whatever you want to call them, they didn't win that night," said Marlin's cousin, Dorothea Moore, "because of a strong black woman who said, 'I'm not afraid of you.' "

But the threat didn't go away. The family packed up and escaped to Oklahoma and eventually to South Omaha, where they joined a meatpacking empire. The Big Four — Armour, Swift, Cudahy and Wilson — recruited the biggest, toughest workers they could find, whether from Poland or Mississippi.

When the Omaha Stockyards became No. 1 in '55, the overwhelming majority of blacks — about 20,000 — lived on the Near North Side. But another 2,000 lived in South Omaha, mostly up the hill from cattle in the Southside Terrace projects. They walked to work.

Marlin Briscoe in 1963.

Home for Marlin Briscoe, his mother and little sister was 2834 S St., where the boy occasionally found a fugitive cow chewing grass in his front yard.

That door was his destination at 9 or 10 years old when he sprinted off the schoolyard, chased by a bully. They dashed into the cluster of matching two-story brick buildings, to the far corner of the complex, the black section. Marlin hoped to see his mom, but the door was locked.

Thump, thump, thump.

His mom looked out the window, saw her boy and the bully. She turned away. Geneva Briscoe raised her son to stand up to a fight.

Marlin and the bully threw a few awkward punches, settled their score and eventually became friends. But Marlin received more than a lesson in camaraderie. His cousin — a 24-year-old teacher who worked summers in a packinghouse — heard about the confrontation. He showed up at Marlin's door with a flimsy cardboard box, filled with old balls and gloves, coated in dust.

The newly-opened Southside Terrace homes in 1940.

I'm going to teach you to play these sports, Bob Rose said.

Remember that name. Over the next 15 years, Rose becomes a huge figure in the black community. The heir to Josh Gibson, mentor to the Sayers brothers, Johnny Rodgers and hundreds of other teenage athletes. But that day, Rose was just trying to give a fragile kid a start.

Neighbors must have thought Marlin was nuts the first time he laced up his black hightop shoes, grabbed a football from the box and walked to the corner of 29th and S Streets. He locked his eyes on a skinny birch tree and fired a spiral.

Miss.

Chase the ball. Hurry back to his spot. Try again.

Miss.

The faces watching from the windows — black and white — worked as butchers and maids, trash collectors and bartenders, pimps and prostitutes. They babysat Marlin when he first moved to the projects. But they didn't have Marlin's vision.

That birch tree? He pictured it wearing a Baltimore Colts jersey, No. 82, split end Raymond Berry. And he wasn't some poor black kid in Omaha. He was Berry's quarterback, the great No. 19. Johnny Unitas!

Marlin wasn't the only kid dreaming big. In terms of density, the Southside Terrace projects may have been the most fertile athletic ground in the

Marlin Briscoe in 1967.

city. Dick Davis and Mike Green, Nebraska running backs in the late '60s, grew up a few doors apart. Dwaine Dillard went on to play for the Harlem Globetrotters. But those positions were integrated. Quarterback was not. White coaches considered it too complicated for blacks.

Briscoe's quarterback teacher in the projects was Ron Kellogg, whose son later shined in the Final Four for Kansas — and whose grandson played quarterback at Nebraska. Kellogg, a teenager at the time, invited Marlin to play tackle football with the older kids. And when it came time for Marlin's first Pop Warner tryout, Kellogg and friends walked him eight blocks to Christie Heights Park.

Entering the white neighborhood risked a fight, but Marlin's escorts wanted to see if he'd get a fair shake. Sure enough, he showed off his skills and earned a spot at his chosen position.

"Not one time did they call me a black quarterback. I was a quarterback."

One day, Rose stopped Rodney Wead on the street and called him to his car. They took a ride to South Omaha and watched Marlin scramble sideline to sideline in a midget football game, making throws with both hands. "I just couldn't believe what I saw," Wead said.

Briscoe's cardboard container of toys — the gift from Bob Rose — withered away. But years later Marlin gave it a nickname:

The magic box.

Back on the kill floor, the temperatures soared past 100 degrees. The blades were so sharp — the work so relentless — that 20 percent of employees suffered a disabling injury every year. The slightest concentration lapse or mechanical flaw might sever a finger or hand.

Lew Garrison was a 120-pound teenager when he got a job on the kill floor, carrying chains from the end of a conveyor back to the start.

"I think it took me two weeks before I could eat lunch," Garrison said. "You've got all this blood and stuff on your clothes. You can wash your hands, but you're still covered with it."

Once the animal had been whacked, knifed, decapitated and skinned, meat surgeons went to work on lower floors, slicing choice cuts, removing organs, wasting nothing. Women filled gruesome processing jobs, packing intestines, collecting blood, boiling bones, cleaning guts.

The pace never stopped. The next chunk of meat was always on its way from the floor above. Workers slipped on wood floors coated with animal fat. They scorched their hands on processing ovens. A flogger suffered a broken foot when a steer stepped on him. Cow urine spilled into another man's work boot, freezing throughout the day and producing frostbite.

Perhaps the worst job of all was underground. The hide cellar. That's where Bob Gibson and his best friend, Rodney Wead, worked one summer during college. Wead's father, a packinghouse veteran, got them jobs. They hauled manure and body parts they didn't care to identify. They salted 100-pound hides and stacked them. Eleven hides per wheelbarrow.

Dave Rimington

Emile Rimington worked the bacon press at Wilson packinghouse for 32 years. Enough to put food on his table. Not enough to send his son to college.

When his son became an all-state offensive lineman at Omaha South in the late-1970s, Emile didn't mince words.

"I hope this football thing works out for you, because I got nothing."

Dave Rimington received a Nebraska scholarship and eventually the Outland Trophy in 1981 and '82. He may be the greatest college center ever. He's also a testament to South Omaha's punch-the-clock culture.

Packinghouse jobs formed the backbone of the black community, but white families needed them, too.

Rimington's mom and dad both worked at Wilson, where they met in the early '50s. Dave grew up at 41st and Drexel Streets, less than 2 miles from the stockyards, surrounded by tough laborers often living paycheck to paycheck. "There was no calling in sick," Rimington said.

Work ethic filtered down to kids. South Omaha produced Golden Gloves champions, professional wrestlers and football standouts, most notably Husker legend Tom "Trainwreck" Novak. Like Rimington, they grew up in the shadow of the packinghouses.

"Everybody around you did an honest day's work," said Rimington, now president of the Boomer Esiason Foundation in New York. "You hang around guys like that and it becomes what you expect.

"There's no excuses."

Armour Packing Plant skinning tables in 1957.

"Slave work," Wead said.

One day an older co-worker — a full-time employee — put one hide too many on the barrow and Gibby, a standout athlete at Creighton, protested. They bickered back and forth until Gibson took his 1,200-pound load, dumped it and quit, the chip on his shoulder as sharp as ever.

Every day at 4 p.m., workers staggered outside in search of relief. Men 25 years old looked like they were 40, Garrison said. Some headed home and tried to shake the odor, immediately shedding their clothes and taking a bath. On payday, they cleaned up and hit the North 24th Street stores. You could tell a packinghouse worker by his strong handshake, his Stetson hats and Stacy Adams shoes. Wead aspired to own those brands.

"To this very day, I wear Stacys."

But some delayed the ride home and headed for the red-light district. South Omaha was "a curious mixture of honest labor and whispered sin," according to one writer, and the packinghouses, like the steel mills of Ohio, anchored a web of taverns, pool halls and nightclubs. Prostitutes occupied street corners, waiting for payday. A bar owner didn't dare close early on Friday. Nor did he deny a butcher a beer based on the color of his skin.

South Omaha wasn't immune to discrimination or segregation. And fights for packinghouse jobs divided ethnic groups in the 1910s and '20s. But by the 1950s, unions were integrated and merit usually determined the best jobs. Packinghouse workers shared an identity — a bond of mental fortitude and physical exhaustion. White, brown, black, didn't matter.

They all smelled the same.

***

John Beasley never forgot his introductory scene. The Tech High grad — and future Hollywood actor — had just left the military when his brother drove him down 24th Street and dropped him off at the packinghouse. Beasley waited in the office for his supervisor, lunch sack in hand, when he saw a dead cow roll by on a cart, its head hanging over the side.

"I go back out the door and I flag down my brother. Hold on! That was my first and last day, man."

Briscoe wasn't so lucky. Like Gibson, he eventually served his time. He experienced the horror of the kill floor — the sledgehammer revolted him. But the hide cellar, Briscoe said, separated the men from the boys.

"The rats down there were as big as dogs."

Briscoe attended South High with classmates who didn't see a way out of the projects via books or balls. They got packinghouse jobs as 11th-graders, liked the smell of a paycheck and never graduated. For him, the packinghouse was something different. A reminder of what awaited him if he quit sports. A driving force to break out of the box.

"I guarantee you, that let me know I needed to go to college."

A generation earlier, blacks didn't have scholarship opportunities. But by 1963, Briscoe had shown enough promise in football and basketball to earn a full ride to Omaha University. He spent the next five years racking up points and accolades. Every May, he returned to his neighborhood's vital industry, never considering it might go away.

In '68, even after the Denver Broncos drafted Briscoe, he lugged beef carcasses three days a week, midnight to 7 a.m. When it finally came time to leave town, the hide cellar took notice. Here was a kid with no father and no money receiving a chance to get out. How would everyone react?

Briscoe got called to the Workmen's Club off Q Street, right between Armour and his front door. He walked in and saw the faces who looked out on his birch tree. The men and women — black and white — who taught him to shoot craps in the taverns, dance in the courtyards and fight in the streets. He was their blood brother and they had a parting gift for him.

A $50 savings bond.

At Omaha University, Briscoe passed for 4,935 career yards, rushed for 1,318 and accounted for 52 touchdowns.

Chapter 4

Sundays at the Park

THEY CLEANED THEIR dinner plates, swapped church clothes for sweats and hustled to the park where The White City once shined.

Then Omaha's greatest generation of athletes divvied up teams and spread across an open field sprinkled with divots and cockleburs.

Who's kicking off?

Thousands of football fans flocked to Tech High and Central on Friday nights in the late 1950s and early '60s, but the real proving ground was Sunday afternoon at Kountze Park. No fans necessary. Pickup football games featured a collection of high school stars, many of whom later played on Sundays in NFL stadiums.

Leslie Webster, who would lead Iowa State in rushing in 1966, got angry one day at Dick Davis, who'd lead Nebraska in rushing in 1967. Davis' response: *I don't fight!* Especially not someone bigger and older, someone he admired.

But Webster came after him, and Davis, a wrestler, took him down. Webster attacked again. Davis flipped him on his back.

It was never too cold for hoops at Kountze Park.

"I learned that day I'm as good as anybody," Davis said. "I just have to play."

Kountze Park was the rite of passage. A testament that iron sharpens iron. Between unmarked boundaries, unpadded teenagers like Gale and Roger Sayers collided at uncomfortable speeds as little kids like Johnny Rodgers fidgeted on the sidelines, aching for a call-up.

"If your good friend was all-state and your cousin was all-state and the guy down the street was all-state, you're gonna want to be all-state," said Preston Love Jr., a 1960 Tech graduate who started at Nebraska. "The whole thing fed on itself. Everybody wanted to be great."

It wasn't just football. On the north side of the park, the games on concrete basketball courts proved just as fiery and almost as physical. Even NBA veteran Bob Boozer showed up on occasion.

"It was a Who's Who," said Marlin Briscoe, who frequently walked six miles from South Omaha to get his Kountze Park fix.

Those few years bridging the Eisenhower and Kennedy eras represented the golden age of the neighborhood. A network of youth coaches and mentors worked day and night teaching lessons. College scholarships finally opened to the best athletes. The first stars — Boozer and Bob Gibson — broke through on a national stage.

The big picture looked promising, too. Omaha's beef industry thrived. The civil rights movement inspired hope. The whole Near North Side hummed.

"The density of North Omaha at the time," said Rudy Smith, former World-Herald photographer, "I've never experienced another place like it."

On weekdays after school, two tributaries — one from Tech, one from Central — converged at 24th and Cuming Streets and formed a bustling river of letter jackets and swing skirts into the neighborhood.

Come weekends, summer especially, the flow never stopped. Cannonballs at Kellom pool. Sock hops at St. Benedict's. Corvette gazing at Jones Body Shop. Picnics at Carter Lake. Banana splits at Reed's Ice Cream. Carnation Ballroom concerts with James Brown or Chuck Berry. Even rock 'n' roll didn't top Easter Sunday, when North Omahans dressed to the nines and paraded down 24th Street.

"I don't care how poor you were," John Beasley said, "you got your Easter outfits."

North O's music scene

The opening guitar riff strikes like a bolt of lightning, shaking hips, kicking feet and lifting goosebumps. Imagine hearing it for the first time, inside a one-story brick building at 24th and Miami Streets.

"Deep down in Louisiana close to New Orleans, way back up in the woods among the evergreens, there stood a log cabin made of earth and wood, where lived a country boy named Johnny B. Goode ..."

Chuck Berry released his biggest hit March 31, 1958. Exactly two months later, he played it live at the Carnation Ballroom. Tickets were $2 at the door.

Mildred Brown must have been glowing. The Omaha Star publisher, grew up going to jazz shows at the Dreamland Ballroom. In 1948, she opened the Carnation, liquor-free, open to all ages.

The Carnation Ballroom was a popular venue for big-name entertainers.

She booked blues icons B.B. King and Ray Charles. She welcomed rock 'n' rollers like Berry and James Brown, who twice played in '57. Kids walking by the Calhoun Hotel at 24th and Lake Streets stalked their tour buses.

Omaha's location as a railroad hub in the middle of the country made it convenient to performers.

"We in the black community had the money and the firepower to demand they come," Rodney Wead said.

The Ritz Theatre in 1945.

Beasley — the future Hollywood actor — spent weekend nights on 24th harmonizing with friends, imitating The Temptations. If you missed him there, check the Ritz Theatre. Two quarters covered a ticket (25 cents), a strawberry soda (15 cents) and popcorn (10 cents). During "Frankenstein" or "Werewolf," he finished his bottle and rolled it down the incline to the front wall for recycling.

Cliiiing, cliiiing, cliiing, cling, cling ... thump.

That was the Near North Side before its demise. A small town that felt like a family reunion. Kids had freedom to be bold — and a bit naive to history.

On the exact ground they played pickup games on Sunday afternoons, North Omaha once hosted the biggest event in its history, the 1898 Trans-Mississippi Exposition. Gondolas glided across a gleaming lagoon. A crowd of 110,000 stood beneath a 278-foot golden dome and listened to President McKinley praise American conquest in the Philippines.

To the Sayers brothers, that must have felt like ancient times. They were moving too fast to look back.

***

What exactly were the pimple-faced lads of Eppleys midget football team supposed to do? Put more defenders on the field? Their opponent, Roberts Dairy, lined up two brothers in the backfield that Sunday afternoon — Oct. 16, 1955. No. 29 and No. 25 had recently been featured in The World-Herald for their exploits. Now they were gonna kick it up a notch.

The Sayers brothers combined for eight touchdowns en route to their city midget football championship. Roger, a 109-pound eighth-grader, scored from 8, 35, 38 and 20 yards. Gale, a 102-pound seventh-grader, scored from 45, 60, 30 and 33 yards.

Final score: 52-0.

"Imagine," said Love Jr., whose Brandeis team lost to Roberts Dairy 26-0 that fall, "being against the team that had Roger Sayers, the fastest man in the world, and Gale Sayers, who you couldn't tackle."

Like many North Omaha kids in the 1950s, Roger and Gale were new in town.

Their roots stretched deep into the northwest Kansas prairie, where dad grew up in a town founded by blacks after the Civil War. He could have practiced law like his uncles, but he wanted his own life. He moved to Wichita, opened a successful brake shop in his backyard and started a family. Roger and Gale arrived 13 months apart.

But in 1950, grandpa Sayers got sick with prostate cancer. Despite mom's protests, dad sold the house, abandoned the business and returned to the prairie to take over the 360-acre family farm. The Sayers boys were the only black students in a two-room schoolhouse. The town name: Speed.

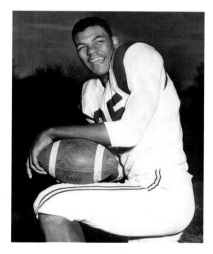

Preston Love Jr. was a three-sport star and all-state football player at Omaha Tech, graduating in 1960.

Grandpa died a year later and his second wife sold the farm. Roger and Gale's dad had nothing to show for his work. "I think he was a little embarrassed," Roger said. "His pride was hurt."

Rather than return to Wichita, as mom wanted, dad called his brother in Omaha and moved the family north. Mom never forgave him.

The family crashed at the uncle's house while dad got a temporary job at Cudahy packinghouse. Roger and Gale's first real Omaha home? The new projects on North 30th Street, where a neighbor introduced the boys to a mind-blowing new picture box. *Television!*

"That's how things were," Roger said. "You could go to your neighbor's house and they'd let some strange kids in to watch TV."

"Lone Ranger" captured their imagination, and for the next decade, Roger and Gale roamed North Omaha like cowboys.

When dad went to work polishing cars at 6 a.m., the boys left the house, too, taking off on their bicycles to Adams Park to climb the hills. They collected pop bottles, turning them in for 2 cents apiece. They took old skates, nailed them to two-by-fours and turned them into skateboards, racing them down Grant Street. When they really craved risk, they built a soapbox and rode down 30th Street from Burdette to Lake.

Look out for cars!

Dad had two jobs and mom cleaned homes. They couldn't afford babysitters, so Roger and Gale — fourth and third grade — had a key to the house. They walked to school and back, finished their chores and hurried outside for another football game in the alley or empty lot. Of course, every latch-key kid lost his key once or twice. Eventually you get smart and pin it to your clothes or hide it behind the house.

The Sayers boys constantly changed keys. They moved nine times in eight years, from one dump to the next. Dad and mom spent much of the rent money on whiskey. They hosted neighborhood poker games. They argued and fought. Four times Mom moved out. Once, they both spent the night in jail.

Where did Roger and Gale find stability? A P.E. teacher at Howard Kennedy grade school.

***

At 19, Bob Rose could've kept his mouth shut. Most Omaha University freshmen would have. But when the men of Alpha Sigma Lambda sang "Old Man River" during a 1950 May Day celebration, Rose heard a lyric that boiled his blood. The N-word.

Remember Rose? The man who introduced little cousin Marlin Briscoe to a magic cardboard box of basketballs and footballs?

Rose came from the same fearless gene pool. In the '40s, his mother picketed Omaha's largest packing plant until Armour hired its first black women. Decades later, she waged a campaign to make Malcolm X's birthplace a national landmark. Rose's father wasn't around, so his mom sent him to Boys Town, where he flourished as an athlete. Rose twice led the Omaha U. basketball team in scoring. He dabbled at quarterback on the gridiron. And he didn't tolerate racial epithets.

Bob Rose as a 6-foot-1 senior at Omaha University in 1953. Rose twice led the team in scoring.

Following the May Day song, Rose and four students complained, prompting a public apology from Omaha U. President Milo Bail.

After earning his degree, Rose got even busier. He starred on Josh Gibson's Omaha Travelers. Dominated the neighborhood free-throw contest. Lifeguarded at the new Kellom pool and made "five daring and skilled rescues." Sold insurance and worked summers at the packinghouse. But like Gibson, Rose's education wasn't enough to coach or teach at a high school — OPS didn't hire blacks.

He settled for coaching the Sayers brothers at Howard Kennedy grade school, introducing them to track and field. During one race, Gale kicked off his shoes — a couple sizes too big — and still caught the leader.

Flag football best highlighted their talent. In 1955, the same season Roger and Gale torched the midget circuit, their Howard Kennedy team outscored opponents 153-8. The next year, they went a little easier on foes: 127-13. Coach Rose called tricks that didn't fly at Omaha U., including a double reverse touchdown pass to Vernon Breakfield on the first snap. Rose was never satisfied. He called practices before school and sent kids home when they goofed around. His term of endearment?

"Sad sack," Beasley said.

"Sad sack," Love said.

"Sad sack," Davis said.

"When he thumped you upside the head and called you sad sack," Briscoe said, "that meant he saw something in you."

Rose's football lessons included an unusual cutting technique that promotes balance. At full speed, plant your right foot and swing the left foot all the way across your right thigh, so you're leaning away from the defender.

"We called it the cross-over," Briscoe said.

Roger (left), Ronnie and Gale Sayers in 1960. The youngest brother suffered from rheumatic fever as a kid and couldn't play football until his senior year at North High. He still earned a scholarship to Omaha University.

Dozens of Rose's pupils practiced it. At least three perfected it: Briscoe, Gale Sayers and Johnny Rodgers.

Mr. Rose opened his home to the Sayers brothers. He took them to Creighton basketball games to watch the only black player on the court: Bob Gibson. The message: *Keep working. You'll make it.* They needed the encouragement because life at home only declined. As soon as Roger, Gale and little brother Ronnie got comfortable in a bedroom, they left it.

"I really hated to move," Roger said. "Seemed like every time we got settled, we moved."

They lived in so many neighborhoods, they learned the fine details of North Omaha's black hierarchy. Kellom and Long Schools were the heart of the ghetto. Howard Kennedy, on the west side of the neighborhood, was almost exclusively black and stocked with packinghouse families.

North of Lake Street, blacks were better off. "They could afford fathers," Beasley said, only half-kidding. Those dads tended to have better jobs, like skycaps at the airport. Their kids attended Central instead of Tech. And they frequently had lighter skin, Roger Sayers said.

"They had it better. They knew it. You could feel it."

Little by little, the black boundary moved north. In 1950, Lothrop School was 80 percent white. Six years later, it was almost 60 percent black. In search of better homes, blacks pushed closer to the old mansions surrounding historic Kountze Park.

On that land in 1898, 2.6 million visitors flocked to the "White City" at Omaha's version of the world's fair.

Midwesterners strolled down eight square blocks of majestic faux-buildings, marveling at Middle East dancers, fortunetellers, ostriches pulling carriages, babies sleeping in incubators, Buffalo Bill's Wild West Show, an Indian Congress featuring the real-life chief Geronimo and an old Southern plantation, where tourists could experience the "old black aunty and the little pickaninny." It all surrounded a grand lagoon that eventually became Kountze Park.

The Trans-Mississippi Expo catered to the common man, but once it ended the neighborhood sought to keep him out. Kountze Place stood for exclusivity, partly because of its brilliant mansions and partly because of its race-restrictive covenants.

In the 1940s and '50s, the area became a battleground as black families tried to integrate the neighborhood.

Black families tried to integrate the wealthy Kountze Place neighborhood.

1898 Expo at North Omaha's Kountze Place

From the city's founding through the 1880s, North Omaha featured a collection of estates and acreages outside the city limits. Then Herman Kountze raised the bar.

The president of First National Bank gobbled up 160 acres of farmland and laid out prestigious "Kountze Place," where the city's richest doctors, lawyers, politicians and businessmen would construct Victorian mansions and commute downtown via a brand-new streetcar line.

The idea seemed lively until the economy collapsed. Drought and depression smacked Omaha in the 1890s and a new political champion emerged.

On July 4, 1892, William Jennings Bryan and more than 10,000 national members of the People's Party held their first convention in North Omaha. From a coliseum on 20th and Burdette Streets, they launched the Populist movement.

Wait, 20th and Burdette? That's the same land where Bob Gibson fielded ground balls from his big brother. The same land that hosted the Coal Bowl each Thanksgiving.

It's always been a small world in North Omaha.

Back to Kountze. In an effort to boost the city's economy and rally citizens, Omaha leaders pitched a world's fair-type event. Back in 1898, Herman Kountze offered 200 acres of fine pastureland north of Omaha if the city would install streets, sidewalks and gas lamps, thus helping him sell lots.

The Trans-Mississippi Exposition was born.

A prominent Omaha lawyer filed a lawsuit in 1956 against his neighbors and real estate agents, alleging that a property sale to a black family at 1817 Pinkney St. decreased the value of his home one block away. Roy Harrop, like his neighbors, had signed a restrictive covenant in 1946 that property "shall not be sold ... to any person or persons of any race other than ... Caucasians." Didn't matter that the Supreme Court had since prohibited restrictive covenants.

Harrop, who'd previously protested the repeal of a state ban on interracial marriage, claimed in '56 "a nationwide conspiracy aided by its propaganda machine of subversive activities to force the will of a minority group on the majority of white property owners." According to Harrop's attorney, selling Kountze Place homes to blacks endangered whites and gave the neighborhood a reputation "as a place of robbery, rape and murder."

You gotta wonder if Harrop ever stepped outside on a Sunday afternoon and walked two blocks to Kountze Park. He might have seen a heck of a pickup game.

***

As segregationists fought the law, the Sayers family rented a house just down the street.

For half a school year, Roger and Gale walked a mile to Howard Kennedy — until one day Gale got sick. The nurse drove him home and discovered that the family no longer lived in Kennedy's attendance area. The next day, the boys were sitting inside Lothrop School, two blocks from their house but a long way from home.

They said goodbye to Mr. Rose and briefly entered a scene that embodied North Omaha's spirit. Pinkney Street.

Local historians might recognize it from Malcolm X's 1925 birthplace — 3448 Pinkney — but the street didn't truly shine until the late '50s and early '60s. Look at this honor roll of alumni:

The Sayers family lived at 2447 Pinkney. Rodney Wead, the professor and activist, raised his kids at 2437. Jerry Bartee, future Creighton baseball coach and Omaha South principal, grew up at 2453. Future North High track standout Gene Washington raced around the yard at 2433. Willis Warren raised a future police chief (Tommy) and a state legislator (Brenda Council) at 2413. All on the same block!

Stroll west to 2620 and you might find future NASA scientist Isaiah Davis watching the stars. Farther up the hill, future State Sen. Ed Danner tracked politics from 2870. And don't forget the future Heisman winner at 2702.

Johnny Rodgers' first memories of his hometown were the train whistles in the River Bottoms, 10th and Locust Streets. No running water. No electricity. The wind kicked up dirt and aggravated his asthma. A rooster chased him to the outhouse — he's still scared of birds.

But when the Jet was 5, his grandpa got a packinghouse job, enabling the family to move to paradise on Pinkney. In the gravel schoolyard at Lothrop, Johnny played "Last One." The object: Dash from fence to building without getting tagged.

Go!

"That's where Johnny started picking up his moves," Bartee said.

Every Thursday Rodgers' grandma picked him up and they caught a cab to 24th and Q Streets, where grandpa, who couldn't read or write, got his paycheck from Cudahy. Grandma bought her husband a few drinks, but she guarded the check.

"She controlled the money," Rodgers said.

Packinghouse checks paid bills up and down the block, including the Warrens' house. For 42 years, Willis worked at Swift, waking up at 5 a.m., reading his paper as he sipped coffee. More like sugar milk, daughter Brenda said. He came home from meat inspections to find kids running from one house to the next. Rodney Wead's wife had a reputation for awareness, so Brenda's friends dared each other to ring the doorbell and get off the porch before Mrs. Wead answered. "Nobody ever made it."

Sometimes they got braver and threw eggs at convertibles. The spanking started where you got caught, Brenda said, and by the time you got home every adult on the block had swatted your butt.

"We always thought, no one is watching us," said Wead's daughter, Ann. "But everyone was watching us!"

Wead was the biggest man on Pinkney Street — 6-foot-6. The most admired, too. He filled his station wagon and drove kids to Council Bluffs' Playland Park. He coached the softball team at Clair Methodist Church. Boys only — much to the chagrin of sweet-swinging Brenda Council.

"Everybody," she boasted, "knew who was the baddest softball player on Pinkney Street!"

The Davis house at 2222 best encapsulated the culture of Pinkney. Like the Sayers brothers, Dick Davis spent his childhood bouncing from one house to the next. Dad was out of the picture. Mom, not even 5 foot tall, opened the door to the needy and closed the door on all guff.

"Nobody messed with Mary Davis," Dick said.

In high school, Dick got a job sacking groceries for 90 cents an hour at Garden Market next to Kountze Park. Every Friday, he and his brother put their earnings on the table. And Mary used it to feed their relatives.

Dick Davis earned all-state at North High and all-Big Eight as a Husker fullback.

Shouldn't we just take care of ourselves? Dick asked. Why are we worried about cousins?

"That was the hardest slap I ever got," Davis said. "Even in football, I've not been hurt any worse. And it shaped my life. If I'm not a good man — a charitable man — my mom will come down from heaven and slap the s--- out of me."

The Sayers brothers didn't stay long at 2447 Pinkney.

They learned new streets with the help of a World-Herald paper route, which they despised. Flag football records didn't mean anything when Roger and Gale knocked on doors to collect.

"We would deliver," Roger said. "They wouldn't pay their bill."

On Feb. 3, 1958, the newspaper reported the arraignment of a 19-year-old drifter who entered the Lancaster County Courthouse in prison denims, a cigarette dangling from his lips. Charles Starkweather had just finished the most harrowing killing spree in state history — 11 murders.

Sixty miles up the road, Marlin Briscoe remembers a different event from Feb. 3. A benchmark that captivated a generation of black athletes. A surprise detailed on his World-Herald sports page the following day:

Kansas State jolts KU in two overtimes ... Boozer hits vital points, outscores Wilt, 32-25

K-State was no underdog — the Wildcats made the Final Four in '58 — but this was Boozer's college highlight, handing Wilt Chamberlain his only career loss at Allen Fieldhouse. Boozer scored the bucket to send the game to overtime, then another to force double OT, then two more baskets. Briscoe absorbed the news, his mind spinning. This was the same Boozer he'd seen at Kountze Park. Now he was beating Wilt Chamberlain? Suddenly the world didn't seem so big.

"It was like the shot heard 'round the world for Omaha," Briscoe said. "He was the catalyst."

Bob Gibson with the Omaha Cardinals

Boozer became a consensus All-American. Meanwhile, his old friend Bob Gibson traveled the country with America's favorite team.

Gibson finished his Creighton career in March '57. A month later, the Harlem Globetrotters came to Omaha for a spring exhibition. Gibson, joining a college all-star team, entered the game in the third quarter and dazzled the Ak-Sar-Ben Coliseum crowd with four buckets and five rebounds, sparking the upset over Meadowlark Lemon and Co., 79-77.

"The Trotters couldn't find anything to be funny about in this one," according to The World-Herald account.

The Globetrotters were so impressed that they recruited Gibson. The following winter, 1957-58, he roomed with Meadowlark during a 130-game tour. Gibson could've spent the next decade clowning the Washington Generals, but the Trotters goofed around too much for his taste. The St. Louis Cardinals matched his $4,000 salary and Gibby chose spring training.

Bob Gibson was no clown. But was he a great pitcher yet? Not exactly. One of his first games with the Omaha Cardinals, St. Louis' Triple-A affiliate, Rodney Wead and Bob Boozer sat in the stands and watched Gibson's first pitch sail over the umpire's head and clang against the screen. Cy Young Awards would have to wait. Gibson and his pregnant wife bought a two-bedroom bungalow on the west edge of the black neighborhood, just down the hill from Malcolm X's first house. The address? 3116 Pinkney St.

Boozer's Gold

Before Bob Boozer ever dunked a basketball, he dreamed of wearing a gold medal.

But in 1959, the Kansas State senior faced a conundrum. Olympic tryouts were still a year away and the U.S. team didn't accept professionals.

Rather than enter the NBA Draft, Boozer retained his amateur status and joined the AAU Peoria Caterpillars.

That's how much the Olympics meant to him.

Boozer's decision paid off in April 1960 when he earned a spot on arguably the greatest amateur basketball team of all time.

The '60 Olympic team in Rome featured four future Hall of Famers: Jerry West, Oscar Robertson, Jerry Lucas and Walt Bellamy. The sightseeing matched the camaraderie. During tuneups, Boozer — a history major at K-State — played in London, Berne, Geneva and Zurich. In Rome, he "went nuts."

"I had a 16mm camera, and I don't know how many feet of color film I took of all the historical monuments and structures."

When Boozer got lost, he just waited for a bus with an Olympic village placard and hopped onboard.

He never got lost on the court. The U.S. crushed opponents by 42 points per game in eight victories, showing off for the crowds. The mood changed when the Russians showed up.

"They wore that hammer and sickle on their chest," Boozer said, "and you knew from their stare how much they wanted to beat you."

The Americans won by 24.

Boozer averaged 7 points per game in Rome. His only mini-regret came when he stole a ball, drove and dunked. The referee called him for traveling, Boozer argued and got ejected.

"I didn't know the guy could understand English."

Boozer wore his gold medal back to Omaha. And 50 years later, the 1960 legends joined the

Boozer's one-year amateur detour paid off at the Rome Olympics in 1960.

1992 Dream Team in the Naismith Hall of Fame. Boozer attended the enshrinement ceremony in Massachusetts, where he struck up a conversation with the ever-opinionated Charles Barkley.

"We'd have kicked your ass," Boozer told Barkley, according to an interview with John Dechant.

Barkley's reply: Who would defend Magic Johnson? Or Karl Malone? Or Larry Bird?

Then Barkley beckoned the most famous Dream Teamer to double-team the 73-year-old Omahan.

Poor Boozer. He throttled the Russians, but he wasn't winning an argument against Michael Jordan.

***

In June 1958, North Omaha hosted the second-largest convention in the city's history. Fifteen thousand Baptist pastors from around the country descended on North 24th Street, but a 29-year-old from Alabama — and leader of the 1956 Montgomery bus boycott — stole the show.

"Cooperating with an evil is as morally wrong as fighting something good. ... Our ultimate aim is not desegregation from a legal aspect. We seek the kind of integration where men come together willingly, not because there is a law."

Over the next five years, Martin Luther King Jr. returned for occasional speaking engagements, including one night at the Civic Auditorium. By 1965, Dr. King said, "we will see a breakdown of the massive resistance to integration."

Progress seemed inevitable. Both for civil rights and the Sayers brothers.

"Rocket Roger" swept the sprints at the 1958 state track meet, covering 100 yards in 9.8 seconds and 220 in 21.7. Not bad for a 5-foot-6½, 136-pounder.

In June 1958, Martin Luther King Jr. visited the home of Ned Moore at 2011 Ohio St. From left Rev. Ralph Abernathy, Pat Wright Brown, Rev. Shaw, Ivory Johnson, Moore and King.

That fall, Central High's backfield tandem made Benson and Tech feel like the Eppleys and Brandeis midget teams. In seven city games, the Sayers brothers combined for 18 touchdowns, mostly from long range: 75, 67, 62, 60, 45, 41 ...

Roger was named the city's top player.

By then, they'd lived in tough places. On 18th Street, weeks passed in high school without heat in the winter. They cranked up the oven overnight, waking up with gas headaches. Their longest stretch was 2211 N. 27th St., where Gale ate sparrows he'd shot with his BB gun. His mom fried chicken feet — 50 cents for 100.

Neighbors filled the plates they couldn't. Roger and Gale knew which kitchens they could get a meal and which basements they could dance on Saturday night. And when the Sayers brothers passed relay batons under the streetlights, even the hustlers knew to leave them alone. That was the "code of ethics," Cathy Hughes said. Athletes supplied the neighborhood with pride.

"They were to be encouraged, nurtured and subsidized," said Hughes, the future media mogul. "It's a beautiful thing when someone has the ability to be a superstar and you make a contribution."

Roger skipped his senior season of football in order to pursue an elite track scholarship. He might've gone to a powerhouse like USC or Kansas, but he pulled a muscle and landed at Omaha U.

Gale, bigger and stronger, had a different temperament. "Gale played angry," Roger said. As a junior, Gale was the city's top football player. As a 6-foot, 180-pound senior in 1960, he excelled at tailback and linebacker, leading Central to an undefeated season, 7-0-1.

The hottest rivalry was Central-Tech. Kids got along fine on after-school walks, but Friday nights sparked fights. Central kids carried an air of superiority and Sayers did nothing to change the relationship. He dominated Tech in '60, rushing for 106 yards on 10 carries and tossing a 35-yard touchdown pass.

Beasley, a Tech defensive end, recalls getting brush-blocked, turning his head and seeing Sayers already 25 yards downfield. Losing was bad, but yielding bragging rights at the post-game hangout — The Fair Deal — hurt worse.

Roger Sayers during an Omaha Central practice in 1958.

Another diner in 1960, Oddo's Drive-In, offered a double-decker "pookieburger" to high school players who scored a touchdown. Gale ate so many his teammates nicknamed him Pookie.

"Gale's headlines," Don Lee wrote in The World-Herald, "were harvested mostly from slashing, high-stepping, long-striding, hard-hitting, high-scoring runs."

He didn't forget his roots. Before school, Gale visited the brand-new Horace Mann Junior High across the street from Kountze Park, where his mentor coached morning basketball practices.

"He wanted to be around Bob Rose," Bartee said.

Seventh-graders gawked at Gale's multiple letter sweaters — white one day, purple the next — all covered in stars and chevrons. "Like a Christmas tree," Bartee said.

Gale Sayers, left, and Vernon Breakfield were both football-track standouts at Central. Sayers' sweater includes 17 chenille stars. The two larger stars are for his All-America and All-Midwest football selections.

In 1961, Gale Sayers shattered the hurdle and broad jump marks in the Greater Omaha track meet.

In Gale's last high school competition, he engaged in one of the great prep track and field duels of all time. Both Sayers and Lincoln High's Bobby Williams — a future NFL defensive back — entered the '61 state meet at Memorial Stadium among the national high school leaders in the long jump. Williams had edged Sayers by one inch during the season.

Gale grabbed the lead on his first leap, 22 feet, 11½ inches. He improved to 23-3 on his third try before Williams bounded in front in the sixth round — 23-3¼. That's where things stayed after Williams' last jump.

Sayers had one more chance.

He summoned his track coach Frank Smagacz, who'd coached Sayers on the football field, too. Smagacz tweaked Gale's angle of approach, then he offered a psychological tip, laying a handkerchief next to the pit at about 23-6. As Sayers turned his back, Smagacz kicked the target forward another foot.

Gale Sayers long jumping at the 1961 state meet.

Sayers sprinted down the runway, hit the board — "Lift!" Smagacz yelled — and sailed past the state record, past Williams' mark and past the nation's high school mark for 1961. Officials measured twice because they couldn't believe where Gale landed.

24-10½.

In August, Sayers returned to Lincoln and scored four touchdowns in the Shrine Bowl. Every time he stepped inside Memorial Stadium he amazed. Why would he play college ball anywhere else?

But after a long and messy recruiting battle, Gale reneged on his Nebraska commitment and chose Kansas, returning to his dad's home state and stirring all kinds of family history.

Gale snubs the Huskers

To Bill Jennings, the 1961 Shrine Bowl must have felt like a movie preview. Gale Sayers scored four scintillating touchdowns — and made a few crushing tackles at linebacker — as the Nebraska coach watched from the Memorial Stadium sidelines.

"I like the way he went up there on defense and hit a few people," Jennings said.

Sayers was slated to be Nebraska's next star — he might even save the Husker coach's job.

Then it all fell apart.

Sayers had signed a grant-in-aid agreement to Nebraska in June, but his recruiting visit still bothered him. Husker running back Willie Ross hollered at Sayers and teammate Vernon Breakfield to take off their Central letter jackets, nearly starting a fight. At the student union, they attended a dance with 44 black athletes and only two black girls.

Sayers and Breakfield were housed in a dorm basement, where heating pipes clanged and temperature fluctuated. I wouldn't go to this college if they gave us a million dollars, Breakfield told Sayers.

Two weeks before school started, Gale visited Kansas, where KU's top athletes greeted him warmly and showed him black fraternities and sororities.

Kansas had gone 7-2-1 in 1960; Nebraska was 4-6. Sayers thought the Jayhawks would better prepare him for the NFL. He flipped to KU, citing pressure from Nebraska boosters. The news stirred an uproar in Omaha.

World-Herald columnist Wally Provost wrote that Sayers was a product of "the big-time college recruiting madness." The NCAA intervened in 1964 with the "national letter of intent," preventing rivals from recruiting prospects after they signed.

Had the Huskers performed in 1961, whiffing on Sayers would've been forgiven. But Jennings went 3-6-1, earning a ticket out of town. His next job? Kansas running backs coach.

Yes, he got to coach Gale Sayers after all.

Roger Sayers Sr. didn't hide personal regrets from his sons. He also hoped his failure wouldn't confine them. "Sorry it didn't work out for your mother and I," he told Roger, Gale and Ronnie, "but you need to get your education and make something better for yourselves."

By 1962, the Sayers brothers were off and running.

To Sioux Falls, where Rocket

Rocket Roger Sayers, right, remained king of the Omaha University sprinters winning the 60-yard dash in a record 6.1 time in early March 1963.

Roger upset world-record holder Bullet Bob Hayes at the '62 NAIA national meet — 9.5 seconds in the 100-yard dash — momentarily staking his claim as the world's fastest man.

To Stanford University, where Roger competed against the Soviets in front of 72,500 fans, tying Hayes in the 100 meters — 10.2 seconds — but losing in a photo finish. (A leg injury ultimately dashed Roger's Olympic hopes.)

Gale Sayers, center, with parents Bernice and Roger in 1965.

To Stillwater, where Gale busted the Big Eight rushing record in his sixth college game, 283 yards at Oklahoma State.

Their exploits didn't just entertain strangers. They motivated the next round of Kountze Park heroes. Take Mike Green, the future Husker running back, who didn't even think about college until he saw the "Kansas Comet."

"All of us coming up behind Gale Sayers wanted to be the next Gale Sayers."

***

As a kid, Roger Sayers helped his father polish chrome bumpers at a service station off 24th Street. Now the 77-year-old great-grandfather creeps down the same road. Sort of. A harsh winter produced potholes the shape of bathtubs. Hit one of these craters at high speed and you'll kill yourself, Roger says.

He turns east off 24th Street and stops at his family's second Pinkney Street residence — where 2121 used to be. Three families lived in the same house, sharing a bathroom. "It was weird." One day in 1961, at the height of his brother's college recruitment, Roger came home and found a '54 Chevy.

"The University of Kansas had left it. And the funny thing was it had a left-handed gear shift. Gale was left-handed."

Suddenly Nebraska's extra benefit — a '51 Ford — didn't look so impressive.

Roger mostly keeps those memories to himself. Gale doesn't live here anymore and Roger's house is in west Omaha, along the 18th fairway at The Players Club.

Jazz blares from his car speakers as he pulls up to his old stomping grounds, the empty Kountze Park. He hasn't been here in years.

"At my age, there's no reason."

Moments later, Johnny Rodgers joins Sayers for a scheduled photo shoot. The Jet still lives just around the corner. He's played weekly paddle ball for 15-20 years on the Kountze Park tennis courts. Rodgers and Sayers discuss street repairs, Husker basketball and their common mentor, Mr. Rose.

Roger Sayers, left, and Johnny Rodgers in March 2019.

"Did he whip you with his leather strap like he did us?" Johnny says.

"No," Roger says, "I didn't have any problem. I was a good kid."

"I remember Bob Rose telling me to run around the gym until *he* got tired."

"Sad sack."

More than 50 years have passed since they came to this park to sharpen their skills. Their field stretches across the southwest corner, just as you see it now. No uniforms or officials necessary. No crowds, either. Sometimes they didn't even know where the sidelines were.

"We knew how to score," Johnny says.

Roger smiles. "We knew how to score."

Chapter 5

Living with Hate

NEAL MOSSER RUSHED ONTO the NU Coliseum court in a fit of rage, confusion and desperation. Before 10,000 frenzied fans and the best team he'd ever coached, with 1:19 left in the state championship game, he did something out of character.

He dropped to his knees.

Mosser, an ex-Marine who sweated through World War II in the South Pacific, captained the 1948 Husker basketball team when he was 28. He got his degree and then the head coaching job at Omaha Tech, where he helped integrate the high school hoops scene. He built a powerhouse with black players, most notably Bob Gibson and Bob Boozer. But the Trojans always fell short in Lincoln.

On March 10, 1962, Tech was on the verge of a breakthrough, riding standout juniors Fred Hare and Joe Williams, leading all-white Lincoln Northeast 58-53 with five minutes left. Then controversy.

A referee whistled Tech for an offensive foul, but rather than give Northeast the ball out of bounds — as Mosser interpreted the rule — the Rockets received free throws. Mosser protested and got a technical.

58-56.

Four minutes later, Tech clung to a three-point lead when Williams pursued a rebound and got tangled with a Rocket. The same white official, Ron Keefer, charged the Trojan forward with throwing a punch. Ejection. As the ref walked Williams to the bench, Mosser buckled. In his suit and tie, on the same floor he played in college, he pleaded for fairness. The ref T'd him up again.

The 1962 Tech High basketball team.

64-64.

Northeast got the ball out of bounds and made a layup. Tech never scored again. With two seconds left, Mosser crossed the boundary once more, gave the ref a peace of his mind and received a third T.

⋇State Champs — the best in Nebraska ✦
page 20

Lincoln Northeast Is Class A King

✦   ✦   ✦   ✦   ✦   ✦   ✦
An Unhappy Finish to Class A Contest

Police battle to break up fights on floor of Coliseum after Northeast's win over Omaha Tech Saturday night.

Final Buzzer Signals
Start of Many Fights

By Don Bryant

The final gun in the Class A basketball championship game at the Nebraska Coliseum halted cage activity, but it started at least 8 separate boxing matches.

Lincoln Police Lt. Melvin Dirra said: "There was here

braska ROTC Military Police cadets surged through the milling throng on the floor to restore order.

When the game ended, the fans poured out of the bleachers and some charged some Lincoln Northeast players, in-

the dressing room, rubbing a knot on his head.

Peterson said someone took a swing at him with "a bottle, or something."

"I knocked it away and we ran for the dressing room," he said.

After partial order was re-

The Lincoln Journal Star features the fights after Northeast's controversial win.

Lincoln Northeast 68, Omaha Tech 64.

As time expired, fans from Tech and Northeast rushed the floor. The refs dashed to safety. Police broke up at least eight fights, shoving people out the doors. Outside the locker rooms, Tech teammates restrained Hare from going after Northeast's players — the loss ruined his heroic 31 points, a new single-game tournament record. Mosser and Tech Principal Carl Palmquist convened in the Coliseum athletic office, gathering testimony for an official protest.

The furor was just beginning. Letters poured in to Tech and to the state newspapers from fans who had watched on TV.

From Grand Island: "Never in 25 years of watching high school basketball have I seen officiating more disgusting than that exhibition."

From Hastings: "I was hoping for Lincoln Northeast to win but after seeing how the referees used such poor judgment ... I could not help but feel that a terrible injustice had been done."

From west Omaha: "The best team did not win, no doubt due to the color of skin of several Tech players. ... Racial prejudice is not just in the South — it is here."

Local papers quoted a letter from Mosser's brother-in-law: "The rape of Omaha Tech by the Nebraska School Activities Association cannot be erased, forgotten or condoned."

Even the new Husker football coach chimed in. Bob Devaney worried the controversy might hurt his chance at the next Gale Sayers.

"All I've heard from Omaha people since the game is that they'll never send a boy to Nebraska," Devaney said. "We've worked hard to cement good feeling between Lincoln and Omaha, and it all goes down the drain in one night."

The following week, Tech considered withdrawing from future state tournaments or the NSAA entirely. Fans signed a petition to overturn the result and move future tournaments to Omaha. Palmquist met with Omaha principals and ripped open old wounds, venting that Bob Boozer "was called every name under the sun" during the state tournament in 1955. "That's the reason the University of Nebraska lost Boozer."

Seven days after the game, a parade of white men in dark suits returned to Lincoln for a most unusual NSAA hearing — Palmquist alone spoke for an hour and 40 minutes. Four hours after it started, the NSAA Board of Control, whose members came from Milford, Albion, Broken Bow, Holdrege and Alliance, voted 5-0 to confirm the final score.

North Omaha had no choice but to move on.

That night in Detroit, Boozer scored a career-high 26 points in a playoff win. In June, Roger Sayers beat Bob Hayes in the 100-yard dash. In July, Bob Gibson, owner of a nasty new curveball, competed in his first All-Star Game in Washington, D.C. — President Kennedy threw out the first pitch. But off the field, bitterness accumulated.

For years, the power structure — white men in dark suits — had promised progress on civil rights, calling meetings, committees and elections to confront issues like open housing and fair employment. Little changed. Inequality festered.

Then in 1963, a national wave of nonviolent activism spilled out of the South, splashing institutions from Chicago Public Schools to the Lincoln Memorial. Blacks in North Omaha got off their knees, marched into the mainstream and proclaimed the grievances they long had endured in silence.

Tech High would eventually get its state championship. But the angst of '62 — the sense that something had been stolen — never washed away. For North Omaha, the episode became a cautionary tale. A reminder never to trust society's referees. According to Marlin Briscoe, those last five minutes bothered Tech standout Fred Hare the rest of his life.

"That state tournament was etched in stone."

***

The man behind the microphones was only five months older than Coach Mosser. Who knows, they could have crossed paths in the South Pacific during World War II. But George Wallace represented an older world in 1963.

He'd witnessed Martin Luther King Jr.'s bus boycott of 1956. He'd watched federal troops escort James Meredith, a black veteran, into the University of Mississippi in 1962.

To Wallace, the walls were closing in. His views, not King's, were under assault. So on a cold day in Montgomery — 100 years and 13 days after Lincoln's Emancipation Proclamation — the new Alabama governor issued his inaugural address to a cheering crowd.

"Let us rise to the call of freedom-loving blood that is in us and send our answer to the tyranny that clanks its chains upon the South. In the name of the greatest people that have ever trod this earth, I draw the line in the dust and toss the gauntlet before the feet of tyranny and I say segregation now, segregation tomorrow and segregation forever."

Blacks in the South didn't need an explanation of what he meant. They knew the limits on jobs and schools. They knew where not to walk or sit. They knew to avoid eye contact with a white girl.

In Omaha, segregation took a more subtle form. Discrimination was "sneaky," one black woman described it in 1963.

"It's worse here in a way, because they'll tell you there isn't any and then it happens to you."

Little moments of disrespect and embarrassment — at a diner or theater or job interview or open house — instilled mistrust and paranoia, eventually transforming into rage.

"This town is sick," said the Rev. James T. Stewart, a Catholic activist in North Omaha. "I'm not speaking of open sores, either. ... No, our sickness is in the bloodstream — in our inner posture. We are an undemocratic city."

Rev. Rudolph McNair, Rev. John Markoe and Rev. Kelsey Jones lead a quiet march at The World-Herald building in September 1963.

In 1963, inspired by resistance in the South, Omaha Star publisher Mildred Brown and two bold black ministers, Kelsey Jones and Rudy McNair, decided they'd seen enough. They adopted an aggressive, deliberate strategy to tackle discrimination in Omaha. They called themselves the Citizens' Coordinating Committee for Civil Liberties, the 4CL, and they protested institutions from City Hall to The World-Herald to Omaha Public Schools. Their first target would be Omaha's favorite swimming pool.

But before summer arrived, Fred Hare had a score to settle in Lincoln.

Rev. Kelsey Jones speaks with demonstrators July 8, 1963.

***

North Omaha's first basketball phenom scored 50 points in a Kellom League game in eighth grade. Hare didn't practice with his classmates at Tech Junior High — he trained with the high school varsity.

"That's how good he was," said Ron Boone, his teammate on the eighth-grade team. "We only saw Fred Hare on game day."

In Hare's first high school game, he scored three late baskets to edge Creighton Prep. While late-blooming Bob Boozer didn't even make Tech's varsity as a sophomore, Hare's greatness was never in doubt. A stark contrast from his upbringing.

He lived on one of North Omaha's poorest streets, 2416 Caldwell. His father, an Arkansas sharecropper, died when Fred was a baby. Three brothers died in a house fire in rural Missouri. Like Josh Gibson, Fred carried the responsibility of taking care of little brothers — even haircuts. But nothing grabbed his attention like basketball.

Fred Hare (holding nephew Frank Morris) and brothers LeRoy (left), Percy, and Jerry in May 1963. He received World-Herald High School Athlete of the Year, the first one-sport athlete and the first black.

"It was sheer rapture," Hare said. "The bouncing of the ball. The swish through the net."

Hare combined extraordinary skill and charisma with an intense work ethic.

"He was pretty much a loner," said Briscoe, Hare's South High rival. "Basketball was his life — his baby. He worked hard in spite of the fact that he was better than all of us."

In the summer, you'd find him with a 25-pound vest around his chest and 10-pound weights on each ankle. Or jumping rope to tone his legs. Or squeezing rubber balls to strengthen his hands.

"Fabulous Fred" scored 24.9 points per game as a junior, including 82 points at state. Senior year, he was better yet, averaging 26.7. His 30.0 in city games broke Boozer's record. Together with 6-foot-3 forward Joe Williams (20.7 per game), Tech rolled into the 1963 state tournament ranked No. 1 and crushed Hastings and Columbus, setting up a showdown with Prep. This time Mosser didn't have to worry about refs. Hare exploded for 31 and the Trojans buried their demons beneath the Coliseum floor, 91-73.

"I'm still dreaming," Mosser said. "I don't think a team can go through the tournament with 75, 83 and 91 points without me getting up off the bench!"

The good dreams kept coming.

March 22: Hare put on his white tuxedo and bow tie for an "enchanted evening." His classmates, most of them white, voted him prom king.

March 26: Parade Magazine named Hare one of the top 15 high school players in the country — third-team All-America. (The first team included 7-foot sophomore Lew Alcindor, later Kareem Abdul-Jabbar, the NBA's all-time leading scorer.)

March 27: All the major politicians showed up at Tech's championship banquet. Gov. Frank Morrison and Joe Cipriano, the new Husker basketball coach, cornered Hare in the hallway and presented a recruiting pitch.

Hare twice visited Kansas, where Gale Sayers was finishing his sophomore year. Boozer escorted Hare to K-State. But he moved like a tortoise in making a decision.

Meanwhile, down in Alabama, Martin Luther King Jr. didn't back down from George Wallace. In April 1963, he led a protest march in Birmingham and landed in jail. In May, police turned dogs and fire hoses on black child protesters.

Fred Hare with Tech coach Neal Mosser (left) and Nebraska coach Joe Cipriano in 1963.

On June 11, one week after Hare received his Tech High diploma, Wallace blocked three black students from registering at the University of Alabama, literally standing in the doorway. That night, JFK addressed the nation from the Oval Office:

> *"If an American, because his skin is dark, cannot eat lunch in a restaurant open to the public, if he cannot send his children to the best public school available, if he cannot vote for the public officials who represent him, if, in short, he cannot enjoy the full and free life which all of us want, then who among us would be content to have the color of his skin changed and stand in his place? Who among us would then be content with the counsels of patience and delay. ...*
>
> *"It is not enough to pin the blame on others, to say this is a problem of one section of the country or another, or deplore the facts that we face. A great change is at hand and our task — our obligation — is to make that revolution — that change — peaceful and constructive for all.*
>
> *"Those who do nothing are inviting shame as well as violence. Those who act boldly are recognizing right as well as reality. ..."*

Hours later, on a quiet Mississippi street, a civil rights leader and D-Day veteran named Medgar Evers stepped out of his car holding T-shirts — "Jim Crow Must Go" — when a white supremacist's bullet tore through his back.

Evers' three children watched him bleed to death in the driveway.

Eight hundred miles north, a fight was brewing to open a wonderland on the edge of town.

At Peony Park, you could dance under the stars at the "world famous Royal Grove." Feel the rush of roller coasters in the amusement park. Play baseball games and watch concerts and host family picnics. Do it all on the city's western edge, 78th and Cass Streets.

On July 26, 1963, Peony Park allowed blacks to swim in its pool for the first time.

Omahans had been spending summer days at Peony Park since 1919, the same year a mob burned a black man's body downtown. On Memorial Day 1963, the resort named after a field of white flowers opened to another huge crowd. Two thousand swimmers soaked in the spring-fed, sand-bottom lake with "pure artesian water."

Only one catch: whites only.

Unlike during Boozer's childhood, blacks could buy the funnel cakes and corn dogs. They could ride the Ferris wheel and do the Twist. They could even be crowned prom king at Peony Park, as Fred Hare was. But no swimming in the pool.

In June 1963, a black airman from Offutt Air Force Base was twice denied entrance, starting a legal battle over whether swimming pools were covered in civil rights statutes. The furor intensified in July when three cars of blacks were refused entry, leading to small demonstrations outside. Callers protested the protesters, flooding the park office and saying they wouldn't swim if Peony allowed blacks on the beach.

"It's hysteria," the park manager said. "I don't know what to do. It will take someone smarter than me to figure out what to do."

Peony Park closed for two days while it considered solutions. Prejudice does not lie behind Peony's gates, park president Joseph Malec Sr. said, "only simple economics." His business couldn't go broke "for the cause of civil rights."

"Let the people in Washington educate the minds of 160 million white people before they pick on the businessmen," Malec said.

On July 18, Peony Park found a stopgap. It opened again as a private club and staff distributed one-day memberships to whites, but not blacks. Two days later, a letter appeared in the Public Pulse:

> "Omaha has been called the All-American city. ... Now this city has an avowedly segregated 'private club' and can take its place beside Mississippi and Alabama as a blight on the national conscience."

The author? A 26-year-old Creighton graduate named "Ernest Chambers."

Peony asked that the case be dismissed, but the judge didn't buy it. So on Friday afternoon, July 26, about a dozen black high school students, escorted by a lifeguard, were allowed into the pool. "Nobody bothered them," said a white swimmer. "Things seemed to go on as normal."

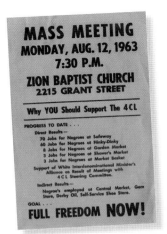

The victory emboldened the 4CL, which pressed the City Council on a range of issues, especially an open housing ordinance. Blacks wanted the right to live outside the walls of the Near North Side.

Ministers Jones and McNair used their North Omaha pulpits to teach methods of peaceful protest — "Do not return hate for hate and hurt for hurt. Whatever the reaction of the white community by way of reprisal, suffer it be so." But the 4CL tactics irked Mayor James Dworak, who called Jones and McNair "yahoos." Demonstrators, Dworak said, were not "caliber people."

During one City Council meeting, blacks stood and sang the national anthem and "We Shall Overcome." The public safety director ordered every police car in Omaha to City Hall, where cops arrested 48 protesters. The following week, the 4CL used the megaphone of the Omaha Star to organize "Showdown Day" at City Hall. McNair proclaimed that "any Negro that can walk, ride or crawl should be there. If for any other reason than sickness or emergency one tries to hold out, they might as well accept the label of TOM because it is true."

The Citizens Coordinating Committee for Civil Liberties (4CL) protested open housing in 1963.

Demonstrators line the balconies of the old City Hall, 18th and Farnam Streets, in October 1963.

The preacher didn't get the whole community, but a massive crowd of protesters — The World-Herald reported 2,000; the Omaha Star said 4,000-plus — converged on City Hall. School kids and senior citizens; Protestants, Catholics and Black Muslims; members of the NAACP and Urban League; the Anti-Defamation League and Inter-racial Council; 150 white people; and even Bob Gibson's wife and girls.

Gibby, who had just finished an 18-9 season with the Cardinals, stayed in the car, worried he might lash out if provoked.

They filled the council chamber, the second and third floors and the main lobby, spilling more than a block outside. Armour closed its hog kill department because so many workers left to participate. This time, the protesters sang nothing. Chanted nothing. Just stood as the council started its 84-item agenda. After an hour, they walked out. The council took no action on open housing.

Gov. Frank Morrison questioned the demonstrators' approach, but he asserted their right to protest.

In August 1963, the March on Washington drew attention to continuing challenges and inequalities.

The 4CL's guiding light was Dr. King.

The last week of August, Omaha barber and activist Dan Goodwin boarded a plane for Washington, D.C., joining more than 200,000 demonstrators on the National Mall. He snapped a photo of Boston Celtics star Bill Russell. He squeezed through the crowd and craned his neck to see King standing in front of Lincoln's statue. *Shhhh.*

> *I have a dream that one day this nation will rise up and live out the true meaning of its creed: 'We hold these truths to be self-evident, that all men are created equal.' ...*
>
> *I have a dream that my four little children will one day live in a nation where they will not be judged by the color of their skin but by the content of their character. ...*

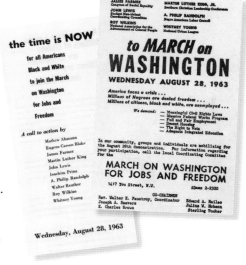

Living with Hate

The March on Washington united Martin Luther King Jr. and President John F. Kennedy.

I have a dream that ... one day right there in Alabama little black boys and black girls will be able to join hands with little white boys and white girls as sisters and brothers.

Eighteen days later — Sunday morning in Birmingham — a 14-year-old girl named Addie Mae Collins stood in a church basement tying the sash of a friend's dress. Dynamite exploded beneath the stairs, killing Addie and three other girls, injuring 22 and interrupting the preacher's sermon plan from Luke 23:34, Jesus' words from the cross.

Father, forgive them, for they know not what they do.

More than 200,000 gathered in front of the Lincoln Memorial for King's "I Have A Dream" speech.

***

Unlike most of North Omaha's best athletes, Fred Hare chose to be a Husker. And he looked like a star from the start.

In his third varsity game, No. 1 Michigan came to the NU Coliseum. All-American Cazzie Russell scored 29 points, but Nebraska rallied from a 10-point deficit with seven minutes left. Trailing 73-72 on the final possession, Hare chased down a loose ball and flipped it blind over his head with one second left. When it dropped, the crowd of 8,500 exploded, rushing onto the court and cutting down the net.

It was ... *rapturous*.

Bob Devaney stopped by the locker room to congratulate the hero, who finished with 20 points. The thrill, Hare said, was about equal to winning the state championship. He led NU in scoring (15.2) and rebounding (7.4) as a redshirt freshman, but Hare's relationship with Cipriano eroded.

"His mistake," Tech High peer John Beasley said, "was to go to Nebraska, a school that didn't utilize his talent. They wanted to change him into something that he wasn't."

Cipriano and Hare butted heads constantly. The coach hassled him to play defense. Hare cited a double standard. Fans just wanted compromise. Hare hurt his knee

Trainer Paul Schneider checks the injured knee of Nebraska guard Fred Hare in January 1966.

as a sophomore and missed the following season — he spent the summer working for the Lincoln Police Department. In November 1967, just as he was making a comeback, his mother died. Maybe that was his breaking point.

One month later Cipriano benched him a few minutes into a home game. Hare waited until halftime, then he walked out of the Coliseum locker room and never came back, joining hundreds of young men in North Omaha saddled with regret.

For every All-American or first-round draft pick, there were 10 great athletes who *didn't* make it because of a scholarship quota, or a school system that didn't prepare them for college, or parents who couldn't feed them, or a coach who didn't like their style, or a city that locked them in a 2-square-mile box.

"There were so many good athletes that were never given the opportunity because of the color of their skin," Boozer said. "Even sitting and thinking about it, you get mad."

Charlie Thomas and Walt Gullie. Johnny Ray and Johnny Alexander. Ernie Britt and Dwaine Dillard. Under different circumstances, those names might have been famous, too. All were talented enough to be professionals and fragile enough to be forgotten.

Gibson, Boozer and Sayers showed North Omaha what was possible. But with no intention, they also widened the gap between those who made it out and those who didn't. The burden of falling short weighed even heavier. In the ghetto, Briscoe said, athleticism was currency and identity. When it wasn't maximized — when it was taken away — young phenoms saw nothing left.

"The disappointment of life hit them and took them out," Briscoe said. "They never did recover. They carried that burden all their life."

Imagine, former Omaha city councilman Frank Brown said, beating a kid from Prep or Westside in high school, yet he gets the ticket to college and you settle for the packinghouse. You read about him in the paper and 25 years later you run into him at a game. He's a doctor and you're stuck.

Fred Hare, left, was the Midwest Athletic Club's Black Athlete of Year in 1963. South High's Marlin Briscoe, right, was runner-up.

"How do you overcome that?" said Brown, who died in 2019.

Hare made it further than most. He earned a few NBA and ABA tryouts. He traveled with the Harlem Clowns. He averaged 35 points per game for the University of Americas team in Mexico.

A head-on collision in 1970 nearly killed him. He returned to Omaha and kept playing pickup games until October '82, when his 18-year-old son was stabbed and killed.

"I had no more desire," Hare said.

He bounced from job to job. When Tech High played its last basketball game in 1984, Hare didn't attend — he hadn't been back to his old gym in almost a decade. He called high school the best phase of his life, something he wished he could relive.

"They're haunting, beautiful memories."

Hare started on a book, "Best of the Best." He wrote tens of thousands of words in longhand, sending them to a local biographer, who typed up and laid out the first 11 pages on his computer. The rest of Fred Hare's story is gone. Lost during a hard drive crash. The book layout shows 90 blank pages. Nothing but white space.

In 2014, Hare died in Texas, unbeknownst to his old teammates, fans and a son who spent five years looking for him. Fred Hare Jr. learned of his father's death two years after he was buried.

"At the very least, I was hoping to hug my dad," he said. "But I've been looking for a ghost."

Living with Hate

x

x

Bob Gibson was in his basement at 3743 Maple St., working on his bar. That's where he learned of President Kennedy's assassination. The next night, Nov. 23, 1963, his big brother's youth baseball team held its postseason banquet at the Near North YMCA. Honorees included the 1950 midget state champions, notably Bob, who addressed the next generation of talent.

Malcolm X speaking in Omaha, June 30, 1964.

The dinner theme: "You got to have heart."

As the nation mourned JFK and a watershed civil rights year came to a close, perseverance and patience still looked good on paper, but darker forces raged fierce as ever. North Omaha was searching for its heart. Its voice.

Then a native son spoke up — Malcolm X.

After white supremacists chased his family out of Omaha in 1926, Malcolm's childhood spun out of control and his rebellion veered toward hatred. His identity and politics seemed constantly in motion. He stood firm, though, for black pride and dignity.

Before the '60s, "Negroes" walked around in a cloud of shame, especially those with the darkest skin. Rodney Wead, the civil rights activist, can still rattle off slogans of inferiority that marked his childhood. *A black cow gives no milk. Bad news is black news. The worst day in American history is Black Friday.* As Big Bill Broonzy sang of discrimination: "If you're white, you're alright. If you're brown, stick around. If you're black, stand back."

Malcolm X confronted the stigmas and attacked the self-loathing. "'Black is beautiful' took off like wildfire," Wead said.

Dr. King was refined; Malcolm X was raw. And during an era of turmoil and disillusionment, he demanded that blacks assert their manhood. He preached not reconciliation but independence. *You don't need them. You're strong enough on your own.*

Of course, the message was frequently lost in translation. Malcolm X criticized Dr. King's tactics — "There's no such thing as a nonviolent revolution." He seemed to revel in JFK's assassination — chickens were coming home to roost, he said.

On June 30, 1964, Malcolm X returned to his hometown at the request of the 4CL. This was two months after completing his pilgrimage to Mecca and two days before President Johnson signed the Civil Rights Act. Down in Mississippi, the feds searched for three Freedom Riders, presumed dead.

Malcolm X had mellowed in '64, breaking from Elijah Muhammad and the Black Muslims, denouncing blanket racism, even building a relationship with his rival, King. But that day in Omaha, Malcolm X was hot. He woke up and sent King a telegram offering "self-defense units" against the KKK in St. Augustine, Florida. "The day of turning the other cheek to those brute beasts is over," he wrote.

Chambers' Letters

The letter does not state the man's age or race. Only the name: "Ernest Chambers."

On Nov. 9, 1953, the future activist and state senator made his debut on The World-Herald editorial page writing — if you can believe it — about the virtue of Christian faith.

That's right. Before Chambers wore his atheism on his cut-off sweatshirt sleeves, even filing a tongue-in-cheek lawsuit against God, he worshipped weekly at Grace Tabernacle.

At 16, Chambers wrote to the Public Pulse:

" 'In the beginning God ...' Stop here a moment. God expects us to believe it because He says it; but man wants to understand. He wants to know where God came from and how, but God will not stoop to satisfy the faithless curiosity of man. He simply says I am, was and always will be. Man is not satisfied with God's word so he substitutes his own theories. He invents the theory of evolution and says God didn't create the Universe, but rather it evolved from a primordial cell. Others tell us it evolved from a fire mist, but these very people who deny God's word can no more explain the origin of the first cell or fire mist. We have no alternative but to accept by faith."

Over the next decade, Chambers' World-Herald letters covered, among other things, Russia, Cuba and weightlifting. He generally adopted the role of peacemaker.

As a Creighton freshman, Chambers participated in a forum at St. John AME Church, where he encouraged people to find a common ground.

"Prejudices start because of a lack of understanding. When we learn to understand other people rather than to tolerate them, then the brotherhood of man becomes a reality."

But as Chambers progressed toward law school and the civil rights movement intensified, his World-Herald letters showed a metamorphosis.

On Sept. 12, 1958, following a World-Herald editorial lamenting division between blacks and whites in the South, Chambers weighed in. "A moral question has no middle ground."

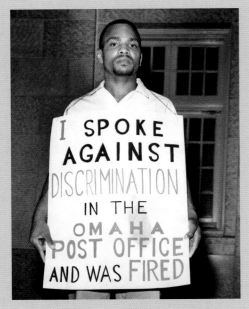

In 1963, Creighton law student Ernie Chambers said the post office fired him as a distribution clerk because he complained that a white supervisor had called him "boy."

On Sept 22, 1958, he responded to a black woman who wrote that she wanted only equal job and educational opportunities.

"I, as a Negro, want considerably more," Chambers wrote. "I want no man, citizen or official, to infringe upon my right to work and live where I choose, enjoy public recreation and entertainment facilities, associate with whomever I choose, and court and marry any girl I can persuade to have me.

By the '60s, Chambers had transformed into a community leader willing and ready to fight the most contentious issues.

"The Negro in America is not free," he wrote on Dec. 28, 1961, "and he is awakening to the fact that he never will be until he stops trying to 'be friends' with the white man. ... The black man must force the country either to accord him his full rights or confess that its intention is to ignore its principles of justice and liberty to grind him under its white heel."

That night, Malcolm delivered a speech to 550 people — many of them white — in a small room at the Civic Auditorium. He reminded them of Omaha's 1919 lynching. During his visit to Africa, Malcolm said, he had seen a blown-up picture of Will Brown burning in front of the Douglas County Courthouse. "When they want to show how a Negro is treated in America," Malcolm said, "they show this scene."

He lamented the history of unpunished violence against Afro-Americans. He challenged society's most intimidating referee — law enforcement.

For years in North Omaha, the sight of police cars elicited a sense of citizen horror. According to blacks, too many cops harassed, terrorized and brutalized not just suspected criminals, but innocent bystanders. Now Malcolm X demanded that blacks, too, pick up rifles and clubs.

"In Omaha, as in other places, the Ku Klux Klan has just changed its bedsheets for policemen's uniforms.

"We have a racist government in Washington that has the audacity to tell us that the South lost the Civil War. The sins of the fathers are about to be visited upon the heads of their children of this generation.

Activist Ernie Chambers inside Spencer Street Barber Shop.

"We do not want integration. We want complete recognition and respect as human beings."

Eight months later, a bullet silenced North Omaha's most famous voice. Black Muslims assassinated Malcolm X in New York City, but they couldn't stop his cause.

At Spencer Street Barber Shop, just a mile from Malcolm X's birthplace, the neighborhood's emerging black radical buzzed hair while executing his real purpose — activating his neighborhood. Ernie Chambers joined Goodwin at Spencer Street in 1965. He covered the shop walls with news articles, photographs and sketches, mostly depicting white racists and brutal cops. But above his barber chair, he posted a personal drawing of a man he revered.

Chambers had read all about Malcolm X. Listened to LP records of Malcolm's speeches.

He admired not only the minister's intellect, discipline and courage, but the absence of hypocrisy — nothing irritates Chambers more than a phony.

They met during Malcolm's Omaha visit and practically finished each other's sentences, Goodwin said. Like one person with two voices. When one stopped talking, the other picked up where he left off. Back and forth for about six hours, deep into the night.

Chambers spent the rest of the 1960s spreading a message that Malcolm X couldn't.

Living with Hate

Chapter 6

Where there's Smoke

BOB GIBSON'S PLANE LANDED at Eppley Airfield just after noon. When he stepped into the sunshine, his 5- and 7-year-old daughters were waiting for him. His wife and mother received bouquets of 31 roses — one for every Yankee strikeout. Tech High students presented him a Trojan pin.

Appearances on Johnny Carson and Ed Sullivan could wait. It was time for a homecoming.

Gibson climbed into a Buick convertible and rode down Abbott Drive. The festivities had been scheduled hastily for Oct. 16, 1964, but word traveled fast enough for spectators to ditch their day jobs and occupy the roadside.

How often do you get a chance to greet a World Series MVP?

Gibson had thrown 10 innings in Game 5, then started Game 7 on two days rest, holding Mickey Mantle and Roger Maris scoreless for five innings as the Cardinals built a 6-0 lead. It was 7-3 after eight innings when Gibson headed back to the mound.

Until that day, one of baseball's enduring racial myths was the fragility of the black pitcher. He wasn't smart enough. He couldn't be trusted in the clutch.

On Oct. 16, 1964, World Series MVP Bob Gibson arrived at Eppley Airfield. That's big brother Josh behind him.

Cardinals manager Johnny Keane, who first coached Gibson as an Omaha minor leaguer in 1958, knew his ace was so sore he couldn't straighten his arm. So why did Keane stick with him, even after Gibson gave up two solo homers in the ninth?

"I had a commitment to his heart," Keane said.

Gibson got the final three outs, becoming the first black player to win World Series MVP.

"Think about what the Yankees were in those pinstripes," said Gibson's best friend, Rodney Wead. "And here comes a kid from Omaha, Nebraska, beating them in Game 7."

Now Gibson stood in front of the Douglas County Courthouse, receiving a key to the city. Mayor James Dworak introduced Gibson's family — including big brother Josh — then designated it "Bob Gibson Day."

Throngs lined the streets during a parade for "Bob Gibson Day." Gibson stopped to toss a ball to a boy.

But looking out at 5,000 people, in *the same place* where white rioters lynched a black packinghouse worker in 1919, Gibson must've wondered — he always did — how many would respect him if he weren't a big leaguer.

Back in the convertible, he rolled north into the heart of his old neighborhood. Past Kellom School and Logan Fontenelle projects. Past the two-bedroom shack where a rat bit his ear, and the rec center where he used to listen to Joe Louis fights, and the old YMCA where he shot line drives in the basement, and thousands of faces he didn't know, but represented. Kids lined the streets with signs, their toes hanging off the curb.

"Kellom School is Proud of You!"

"Welcome Home, Champ!"

"Hi, Bob"

The city stopped that afternoon — just for a couple of hours — and united behind a native son. But the good vibes were a myth. The Near North Side, overcrowded and dilapidated, was losing patience with inequality. Whites accepted blacks on their TV screens. Even cheered them in parades. But living next to them? No.

Meanwhile, cracks within the black community opened, too. Old, cautious and non-violent on one side. Young, progressive and militant on the other.

Within two years of Gibson's parade, the school kids and their signs would be replaced by National Guardsmen holding rifles. North 24th Street would never look the same.

Where there's Smoke

***

Gale Sayers sat against a hallway wall in the Kansas University administration building, scrunched in a crowd.

It was March 8, 1965, two weeks after the Nation of Islam killed Malcolm X and just one day after 400 unarmed blacks attempted to march across the Edmund Pettus Bridge in Selma, Alabama, only to be beaten by police. Bloody Sunday.

Sayers had chosen KU over Nebraska partly because of its racial diversity. But that morning, he and 150 students protested discrimination in university housing and the Greek system. Sayers wasn't beaten, just arrested.

Sayers, back row center, joins fellow Kansas University protesters.

"They accept me as a football star," said the two-time All-American, "but not as a Negro."

As 1965 unfolded, black athletes felt more and more responsibility to stand up. On Aug. 12, the "Kansas Comet" made his professional debut for the Chicago Bears, a preseason win over the Redskins. The same day, inner-city Los Angeles erupted following an ordinary reckless driving arrest.

The Watts riots raged five days, killing 34 people, injuring 1,000 and leading to almost 3,500 arrests. Hundreds of white-owned businesses were destroyed.

Through the 1950s and early '60s, the South anchored the civil rights movement. Headlines came from Birmingham and Oxford, Little Rock and Greensboro.

Suddenly, Northern ghettos emerged as a battleground. Children of the Great Migration felt emboldened to express anger with violence. Sit-ins and protest marches had run their course. "We Shall Overcome" was soon drowned out by Stokely Carmichael's "Black Power."

Sayers didn't make any more headlines on the civil rights front. He was busy shattering standards of football showmanship.

In his third regular-season game, he totaled 184 yards rushing and receiving at Green Bay. Two weeks later in Minnesota, Sayers scored four second-half touchdowns and compiled 324 all-purpose yards on 22 touches, including a 96-yard, go-ahead kickoff return with 2:18 left.

Sayers vomited before every game in '65. Too nervous. But on the field he epitomized grace. During an era of three yards and a cloud of dust, he made football artistic. Tackling him was like catching a bird in midair. He made turns others didn't even see, at full speed.

"He took you by surprise even when you knew he was coming," Packers coach Vince Lombardi said.

Sayers saved his best performance of 1965 for sloppy Wrigley Field. On Dec. 12 against San Francisco, he produced 336 all-purpose yards and six touchdowns on just 16 touches. Mud stained his white pants but didn't slow him down. He scored on an 80-yard screen pass, a 50-yard run and an 85-yard punt return.

"That was the greatest game of football I have ever seen a man play," Bears coach George Halas said afterward.

"The greatest performance in National Football League history," Bears teammate Mike Ditka said decades later.

"I just wonder how many that Sayers would have scored if we hadn't set our defense to stop him," said Hall of Fame quarterback Y.A. Tittle, then a 49ers assistant.

Sayers finished his rookie year with 22 touchdowns, an NFL record. Back home in Omaha, his old friends were impressed but not terribly surprised. They'd seen Gale do the same things on Sunday afternoons at Kountze Park.

***

Bobby Bland played the blues one more time at the Dreamland Ballroom on Dec. 17, 1965. Shortly after, North 24th Street's most famous music hub closed without much fanfare. North Omaha had deeper sorrows.

Meatpacking had fallen on hard times and the latest plunge came at Cudahy, which laid off 470 workers, including 300 blacks. In 1955, when Omaha became the world's largest meatpacking center, the packinghouses employed 12,100. A decade later, it dropped to 7,200. The list of headaches:

- New environmental regulations stymied old methods of waste removal. Packers came to Omaha in part because they could turn the Missouri River into a sewer drain. Now the government demanded they stop.

- Old slaughterhouses cracked and crumbled after 80 years. Maintenance costs soared.

- Automation reduced the need for massive buildings and maximum workforces.

- The biggest problem was new competitors like Iowa Beef Packers, which recognized a better blueprint: smaller plants in smaller towns. They could get free land and tax breaks. They could access cheaper (often non-union) labor in more efficient facilities.

In April of 1965, more than 1,000 union members were fired in a labor dispute at Cudahy Packing Co., eliciting a standing-room-only meeting at the workers union hall in South Omaha.

From 1960-65, 17 plants sprouted across Nebraska and southwest Iowa.

In Dakota City, Nebraska, IBP slaughtered four times as many cattle (per man) as Armour in South Omaha. Machines moved, sealed, weighed and stamped boxes, then transported pallets to trucks. One man at a control panel could operate an entire rendering plant, turning animal waste into soap and tallow.

The new way appealed to farmers, too. They didn't have to spend a day waiting in line on L Street. Nor did they have to share profits with commission agents — they cut out middlemen.

In 1925, 91 percent of cattle sales happened at terminal markets like Omaha's. By '64, it was 36 percent and plummeting.

"There no longer is a reason to pay the higher costs of having a meatpacking plant in a big city," IBP executive Maurice McGill said. "We foresee a day when thousands of head of cattle are fed in gigantic feed lots located near small, highly automated packing plants."

"The Davids," The World-Herald's Bob Dorr wrote, "are killing off the Goliaths."

As the Big Four — Armour, Swift, Cudahy and Wilson — strained to modernize, Omaha officials did their best to minimize doom and gloom. They called a 17 percent decline in total livestock receipts in '65 a temporary setback.

"The future of the stockyards will be greater than its past," said Charles O'Rourke, Union Stockyards Co. vice president.

Some smaller visionaries remained bullish on Omaha.

"The finest meat in the world is in this market," said Lester Simon of Table Supply Meat Co. in South Omaha. "Steaks are more tender and have better flavor because the cattle are fattened on corn."

In May 1966, Simon, his three sons and 50 employees moved into a new (non-slaughtering) plant at 96th and I Streets. Sales immediately exploded, prompting a company name change. You may have heard of it:

Omaha Steaks International.

***

Nebraska beef gained worldwide fame, but North Omaha didn't taste the benefits.

Blacks suffered a disproportionate percentage of job loss and these were no ordinary jobs. The average packinghouse worker made $3 an hour, about $23 in today's money. Some highly skilled workers, like ham and beef boners, could make $10 an hour, or $78 today.

Cathy Hughes' 25-year-old husband supervised the kosher kill at Cudahy. His all-black crew worked without the benefit of a sledgehammer. They wrestled, shackled and hoisted conscious cattle upside down — "It was truly a rodeo," Hughes said. Then a rabbi slit the cow's throat.

Friday afternoon, her husband received his paycheck, stopped at the post office and bought their new baby boy a $50 savings bond, purchased for $37.50. Week after week after week. Hughes eventually counted $2,000-3,000 worth.

"Who would've believed that was going to end?" Hughes said.

Most fired workers had no experience outside the packinghouse and no education. Eighty percent of Cudahy layoffs in '65 hadn't graduated high school; 75 percent were 45 or older. They didn't want to go back to school, nor did they want to learn new skills. Even when they did, other manufacturing unions didn't hire blacks as equally as meatpackers did.

"It takes a great deal of counseling simply to get people to accept their plight," one labor official said.

North Omaha's "plight" was supposed to improve with civil rights. Instead, conditions further deteriorated. The non-violent 4CL lost influence as more aggressive voices, especially Black Muslims moving to the neighborhood, swayed youth.

"Omaha has a very explosive situation," a human relations board member said. "I think any form of self-delusion is dangerous as hell."

The fuse lay waiting in a grocery store parking lot at 24th and Lake Streets. In 1964, a Safeway opened at the northeast corner to great fanfare: "The store of tomorrow ... here today!" advertisements declared.

But the parking lot, which featured 180 stalls, soon became a popular after-hours hangout. Gamblers shot dice. Drunks broke bottles. Pimps and prostitutes conducted business.

To discourage loitering, Safeway stretched a single chain around the parking lot. Blacks protested the makeshift fence and the store removed it.

The Safeway grocery store at 24th and Lake Streets in April 1965.

"Negroes hate chains," the Rev. General Woods said, "whether they are around a black man's legs on a Georgia chain gang or around a white man's supermarket in Omaha."

By '66, whites didn't feel welcome in the supermarket — or on 24th Street — after dark. But philosophically the neighborhood sustained its diversity.

When Mayor A.V. Sorensen lamented that blacks needed to "get together and agree upon what they want," a black writer named Douglass Hall called him naive:

> *The Negro is many: white and black, dirty and clean, diseased and healthy, beautiful and ugly, smart and lazy, sad and happy, brilliant and dumb, Democrat and Republican, Catholic and Protestant, sinner and saint.*
>
> *He loves beer and iced tea, milkshakes and martinis, spare ribs and spinach, jazz and hymns, Bach and the blues.*
>
> *He steals, begs, bleeds, fights, loves, feels, runs, jumps, works, prays and sings.*
>
> *That Negro over there wants "Freedom Now" and this one here is willing to wait, and the Negro in the corner does not really care about freedom at all.*

All true. But in '66, the neighborhood's most eloquent voice presented only the militant point of view. From his barbershop at 24th and Spencer, atheist Ernie Chambers preached the gospel of oppression.

When police meet white folks, he said, they smile and remove their hats. But on the Near North Side, he said, they approach every black woman as if she's a prostitute and every black man as if he's a thief.

Police brutality, Chambers said, isn't just physical head whipping. It's constant agitation and disrespect. How could North Omaha open the city's eyes to injustice?

"A bomb is the only answer," Chambers said. "Someone will have to blow up downtown Omaha to convince the white power structure that we mean business — that we are sick of imprisonment in this ghetto."

***

The civil rights movement was spinning off its axis, but North Omaha still had a moral compass. A coach who regularly advertised for opponents on The World-Herald sports page.

Josh Gibson of Near North YMCA (341-9134) is anxious to schedule post-season games with Legion and midget baseball teams in Southwest Iowa and Eastern Nebraska.

Coach Josh Gibson's YMCA team circa 1962.

Josh was feisty as ever, even if his catcher's mitt was older than his players. "He'd pounded that glove so much," said one of Gibson's players, Al Gilmore, "that thing was almost like a handkerchief." Occasionally after he crossed an umpire, Josh pulled his team off the field and forfeited. Once after a loss, he made his kids walk 6 miles from South Omaha's Brown Park, pointing north.

Just keep going straight. You'll make it home.

"South Omaha was a long-ass way," said a speedy center fielder named Johnny Rodgers.

The Sayers brothers. Marlin Briscoe. Ron Boone. They all played for Josh. They all experienced his wrath, his lectures and his lessons about conserving wooden bats.

Don't use the bats to smack mud off your cleats. Use these instead — popsicle sticks.

Sometimes Bob Gibson stopped by practice and pitched to them. Sometimes teen girls like Cathy Hughes stopped by and Josh pointed them home. "You all need to get away from here. Little fast girls!"

In the winter, Josh welcomed the new Husker football coaches to watch his YMCA basketball leagues. Bill Jennings never bothered, but Bob Devaney sat in the bleachers and looked for talent. Josh used it to motivate his kids: *You're not forgotten here. Do the right things and you'll succeed.*

After league games, Josh caught a ride home from his brother Fred, stopping the car when he saw familiar faces on the street corners.

"He would actually make them get in the car, ream them out and take them home," said his nephew Fred Jr., who watched it all from the back seat. "People loved him and hated him at the same time."

In the spring of 1966, a group of Gibson pupils took their popsicle sticks to Tech High, which had never won anything in baseball — they didn't even have a place to practice. The best Trojan athletes opted for track and field, saving baseball for the summer.

Tech's 6-5 record entering the district final pleased coach John Morse. Then it clipped Omaha Westside 3-2 to earn a place in the state tournament bracket.

At Rosenblatt Stadium, Phil Wise's two-run triple in the fifth inning broke Lincoln Southeast and moved Tech into the state championship game against Benson.

Underdog Tech celebrated a state title in 1966. From left, Bobby Griego, Roger Ulmar and Phil Wise.

Coach Morse, a white Benson grad, caught for Bob in semi-pro ball — his hand swelled so badly that he padded his mitt with a sponge. Morse graduated college and landed at Tech in '58, teaching P.E. and history — "Josh should've probably got the job that I got."

As Morse prepared the Trojans for the state championship game, Bob sifted through memories at 3743 Maple St.

His new entertainment center had caught fire and spread to his family room. He got a call from his wife, flew home between starts and found his trophies and awards destroyed.

The ball from his first major-league win in 1959? Gone. The ball from Game 7 of the '64 World Series? Gone.

Gibson cleaned up the past, flew back to St. Louis and — one day later — pitched nine innings to beat the Cubs, 3-2.

He missed his alma mater's finest baseball moment. Roger Ulmar pitched a gem, Wise — the future NFL safety — went 4-for-4 and Bobby Griego's daring steal of home with two strikes and two outs in the fourth inning sparked a four-run surge. Tech beat Benson, 5-2.

State champs.

Nebraska Gov. Frank Morrison introduces President Lyndon Johnson, sitting at left, on June 30, 1966. The Missouri River rolls by behind them.

***

Air Force One touched down at 12:03 p.m. President Johnson greeted Omahans along a fence line. He stopped for just one reporter, the Omaha Star's Charles Washington, who asked about the elusive piece of the president's civil rights package: open housing.

The president expressed confidence that Congress would pass his bill soon. He greeted Bob Boozer and Mildred Brown, the Star publisher, then headed via motorcade to the Missouri riverfront. Shortly before his arrival, the event took an ominous turn. The speaker's stand was engulfed in smoke from nearby trash fires.

The public greets President Johnson before his Vietnam speech in Omaha.

It was 90 degrees when the Boys Town band played "Hail to the Chief." Johnson stepped to the microphone and delivered a major foreign policy speech.

"I'm convinced that after decades of wars and threats of wars, peace is more within our reach than at any time in this century." It was June 30, 1966, two years before the Vietnam War's darkest days.

Where there's Smoke

"The Communists expect us to lose heart," LBJ said. "They intend to wear us down. They believe political disagreements in Washington and confusion and doubt in the United States will hand them victory in South Vietnam — and then in Asia. They are wrong."

At 1:33 p.m., Air Force One returned to the sky, leaving behind the trail of smoke.

Two days later, a crowd of blacks — mostly late-teens and 20s — congregated Saturday night on Lake Street. The pop-pop of fireworks prompted a police call at 12:49 a.m., just as the bars emptied.

Two cruisers pulled into the Safeway parking lot, where about 150 people clustered. The cops attempted to break up the crowd with bullhorns. When they threatened arrests, the heckling started.

One member of the crowd threw a bottle. One tossed a lighted firecracker at the cops' feet. The officers retreated and called for backup. When they circled the block, a bottle smashed a cruiser window. The crowd spilled out of the parking lot to 24th Street, where three stores were looted.

Police returned with 12-gauge sawed-off shotguns and arrested eight people, dispersing the crowd by 3 a.m.

One of four men who staged an impromptu sit-down on Lake Street on July 5, 1966.

Police respond to bottle throwers at a North Omaha apartment house during the 1966 civil unrest.

National Guardsmen formed a wedge shape before moving west on Lake Street on July 4, 1966.

The next night, disturbances continued — Mayor Sorensen estimated 4,000 people on 24th Street just before midnight. On North 16th Street, an off-duty white cop came upon 20 kids looting the Gamble Store. They ran and he shot a 15-year-old kid in the leg.

Fortunately, just the leg.

Store owners camped out with rifles across their laps, awaiting looters. By dawn, the record showed more than 40 broken windows and 50 arrests. Fourteen black ministers condemned the uprisings, which "only lead to the total destruction of our community."

That night, July 4, the scene escalated again. As fireworks exploded around the city, about 100 helmeted officers and troopers dispersed the Safeway parking lot crowd without injury. But it didn't end there.

Within an hour, 44 National Guardsmen marched south down 24th Street from Maple to Lake in V formation — 500 more helmeted troops awaited call at the armory. The 44 marched in silence, their bayonets shining beneath the streetlights. When they arrived at 24th and Lake at 1:40 a.m., the intersection had already been cleared, so they turned west on Lake, where helmeted policemen pursued hecklers — "Whitey!"

Twelve policemen chased a single bottle thrower into an apartment. At another house, cops busted down the door and came out with a man bleeding from his head.

"Both sides are stupid," said a 24-year-old black man watching from his porch. "It won't help a bit."

Where there's Smoke

The mayor tried to mend fences, meeting with black youths to hear their grievances: "Gestapo" cops, joblessness and lack of recreation spots.

Sorensen conceded that cops occasionally brutalized blacks. "Men have deeply ingrained attitudes," the mayor said, "and sometimes you don't change them with just a week's course in human relations."

He reminded citizens that of 30,000 blacks in Omaha, only 200 stirred trouble. Gov. Frank Morrison echoed Sorensen, hoping the situation would "shock the conscience" of Omahans who "neglected for many, many years" the Near North Side.

Truth was, the '66 riots — the city's first major disturbances of the civil rights era — only widened the gap between black and white Omaha. They also split the black community, old vs. young, moderate vs. radical, those who viewed a bottle half full vs. those who'd rather smash it half empty in the street.

Workers at Schollman Hardware cover broken windows with sheets of plywood.

The aftermath of rioting in July 1966 just north of 24th and Lake Streets.

Arsonists started a fire at 1629 N. 24th St. in August 1966.

In August 1966, Sorensen testified in Washington before a Senate subcommittee examining urban violence. He blamed "slumlords" and federal lawmakers for blocking urban renewal funds. He blamed Nebraska's "rural Legislature" and citizens of Omaha for ignoring blacks' problems. Sorensen outlined a bold plan to "break up the ghetto," moving 1,000 families into all-white neighborhoods with subsidized rent and aid from churches and civic groups.

Omaha Mayor A.V. Sorensen speaks at a playground opening at 28th and Grant Streets in August 1966.

"Deplorable living conditions and social unrest go hand in hand. Substandard housing, high levels of unemployment and poverty incomes make family breakdown and social disorder predictable."

America, Omaha's mayor said in the nation's Capitol, should commit as much money to urban cities as it does to foreign aid.

"I would not hang my head in shame if we failed to be first putting a man on the moon but were able to find a cure for this cancer which bedevils our society."

***

On Sept. 11, 1966, Gale Sayers opened his second NFL season with 79 yards on 17 carries — he'd go on to lead the league in rushing. Back home, the state's biggest politicians — and Bob Boozer — gathered on North 24th Street for a public ceremony.

They read official proclamations and presented American flags to inaugurate the new Bryant Center, the finest outdoor basketball playground in Omaha, complete with five blacktop courts, lights, bleachers and an electric scoreboard.

Eat your heart out, Rucker Park.

St. Benedict's built Bryant Center on an empty lot at 24th and Burdette, right next to the Omaha Star. Prime real estate. Immediately it became a magnet for competition and socializing.

"That's where the boys were!" future state senator Brenda Council said.

"Your mothers would be looking at you strange because that's when we dressed up the cutest," future media mogul Cathy Hughes said. "We got our hair done to go stand out in that heat. On the fence. And watch the guys play. That was like watching the all-star game to us."

Bryant Center, an outdoor basketball facility, officially opened on Sept. 11, 1966. St. Benedict's built it on an empty lot at 24th and Burdette Streets, right next to The Omaha Star.

Ron Boone

You never knew who might show up at Bryant Center. In 1969, Marlin Briscoe walked in with his new friend from the Buffalo Bills, O.J. Simpson.

"Biggest head I've ever seen in my life," said Council, who knew O.J. was trouble when he reeked of marijuana.

Bryant Center's biggest regular star was Ron Boone, who dribbled his ball from 25th and Sprague, where his single mother fed six kids. That was nothing — there must have been 60 kids on their dead-end street.

When an unknown car turned south down 25th Avenue, failing to recognize the dead end, kids playing baseball in the street grumbled and glared.

In high school, Boone hitchhiked to Tech, saving his bus money for a burger, fries and Coke at McDonald's — "All three of those things. 37 cents." After school, he dribbled his ball to Kountze Park, shoveling snow off the concrete when necessary. But Boone was no phenom. He rode the bench in '63 as Fred Hare carried Tech to the state championship.

The next year, Boone averaged 12 points per game as a senior and landed in junior college. That's where he grew 4 inches. He earned a scholarship to Idaho State and blossomed into a pro prospect. But Boone always came home for the summer.

"One day at Bryant Center," Briscoe said, "he dunked on me like Blake Griffin. I couldn't believe it was the same little kid. He said, 'Now *that's* for all those years.'"

Roger Sayers' Bears tryout

Of the countless audacious ideas hatched inside Spencer Street Barber Shop over the years, this one ranked among the wildest.

In May 1966, Ernie Chambers and Dan Goodwin took a break from civil rights and crafted a letter to legendary Chicago Bears coach and owner, George Halas. Their purpose? Get Roger Sayers an NFL chance.

"I went along with the barbershop banter," Roger said in 1966.

The notion didn't come out of nowhere. Gale had just completed his record-breaking rookie year with the Bears. Didn't Halas recognize that Gale's older brother, a 24-year-old Mutual of Omaha underwriter at the time, had rushed for 2,000 career yards at Omaha University? 8.6 yards per carry!

The barbers praised Roger's speed, durability and heart. They suggested that his help on kickoff returns could reduce Gale's injury risk.

"You are not the kind of man to tremble at the thought of looking at a man whose only drawback is 'smallness,'" the barbers wrote. "And as a Coach with an eye trained for such things, you will undoubtedly see more than we have seen. You may be placed in a position to again 'scoop' the rest of the NFL.

"If you have any doubts or questions about all this, you can obtain additional information from one of the greatest players to join the NFL in recent history — Gale Sayers."

It worked. Weeks later, the Bears signed the 155-pound Roger, whose only recent training came from softball and golf. Halas didn't make predictions, but "there have been some great little men in our league."

Roger instantly became the fastest man in training camp. But his transition to flanker proved difficult. Sayers played in exhibition games but failed to make the final cut in late August.

The Bears offered him a practice squad spot, but Roger turned it down and returned to Omaha. "I got pretty close."

Basketball was Briscoe's first love, too. On Sept. 10, the day before Bryant Center's official grand opening, Marlin started his third season at quarterback for Omaha University, coasting through an exhibition win over Nebraska Wesleyan.

Then he drove to Bryant Center for a pickup basketball game. Briscoe was high above the blacktop when an opponent undercut him. Briscoe landed on the back of his head.

The following Saturday, Omaha U. opened at Idaho State. With Boone watching, Briscoe threw for 179 yards and rushed for 73 in a 28-20 loss. But a second hit to his neck knocked the senior captain out of the game and prompted a hospital visit. Doctors diagnosed a fractured vertebrae.

"They told me I was done," Briscoe said. "I was lucky I wasn't paralyzed."

He grabbed a clipboard and coached his teammates, who staggered to a 1-9 record. He rehabilitated on his own time, earned his degree and hoped for a second chance.

***

The mayor came home from Washington, D.C., and pushed reforms to help the Near North Side.

He pitched a summer camping retreat near Columbus, Nebraska, where policemen and black kids shared cabins, fishing poles and horse saddles. He hired Bob Gibson to help establish a police athletic league, and Bob Boozer to lead basketball clinics. He even hired black citizens to help patrol the Near North Side.

Through the list of ideas, a message cut between the lines: It took civil unrest to get the city's attention.

Sorensen's public safety director, Francis Lynch, criticized the mayor for going soft. He called the Near North Side "a jungle." The solution for 200-300 "hoodlums" wasn't stronger programs, it was a stronger hand.

The Carnation Ballroom at 24th and Miami was boarded up by 1967.

"Diplomatic law enforcement is a euphemism for selective law enforcement," Lynch wrote. He accused Sorensen of submitting to blackmail.

Sorensen fired Lynch, but he couldn't restore faith on North 24th Street. For decades, segregation locked blacks inside the Near North Side as white consumers were free to come and go. They visited white-owned print shops, body shops, ice cream shops, even bars and restaurants. After the '66 riots, whites stopped coming down and stores like Tully's, which had been ransacked for $20,000 in merchandise, closed.

Said one remaining merchant: "We treat everyone who walks in as a potential customer and a potential robber."

Property values dropped. Insurance rates skyrocketed — some companies flat-out refused to write policies on the Near North Side. Shopkeepers let their leases expire and walked away, leaving good buildings vacant, their once-gleaming storefront windows covered in plywood.

"It was an eye opener to what was going to happen in the future," Boone said.

He didn't see it coming. In the summer of '66, Boone had just finished his first season at Idaho State. His college coach was on the way home to Indiana and offered to drop off Boone in Omaha.

After 1,000 miles in the car, Boone was anxious to show Coach where he came from. Bad timing. They turned north on 24th Street, Boone said, and drove right into the sirens and smoke. The first riots. Needless to say, Coach didn't stick around for a tour.

"Every time he told the story, he'd say, 'I got Ron out of North Omaha. Otherwise he'd be dead by now.'"

It was a riveting tale — if North Omaha wasn't your home.

A scuffle at home plate

The 1960s social revolution transcended race, gender, class and country. Young people rebelled against institutions, violently demanding change. But resistance didn't happen unprompted.

In April 1966, Central High's all-city shortstop dug into the Boyd Park batter's box. Six weeks later, Jerry Bartee would get drafted by the St. Louis Cardinals, but his talent didn't earn him respect that day. As Bartee took his stance, the catcher called him a racial epithet.

Bartee stepped out. "What'd you say?"

The catcher stood up and said it again. Bartee waited for the umpire to intervene and when nothing happened he started throwing punches. The umpire ejected both players.

After the game, Bartee was walking to his mom's house, angry and disillusioned. A car pulled up and the driver — the umpire — offered a ride. Bartee declined.

"But can I ask you a question?" he said. "Why did you let that go that far?"

The ump didn't answer. The next day, a Central administrator summoned Bartee and demanded to know: What did he call you?

"I wasn't comfortable back then — nor am I comfortable today — using that term to a white guy," Bartee said. "He knew. The coaches told him everything. But he got perverted pleasure out of hearing me say that the kid called me an N-word."

In 24 hours, two white authority figures let Bartee down, prompting more reflection. What if his elders didn't have his best interests? What if they weren't only dragging their feet, but actively standing in the way?

"Can I trust white adults in situations like that to do the right thing?" Bartee remembered thinking. "I knew what the right thing was. The right thing was to let the supervising adult handle the situation. I was taught that. I did that."

Look where it got him. Punished for a grown man's mistake.

Chapter 7

Property Rights

OMAHA?!? WHERE the heck is Omaha?

By 1967, Bob Boozer had played for NBA teams in Cincinnati, New York, Los Angeles and Chicago. His teammates shared something more than long legs: They couldn't find his hometown on a map.

"They laughed at Bob because he loved Omaha so much," wife Ella said. "They didn't even know black people lived in Omaha, I swear."

Ella could relate. The sassy Cincinnati native married her gentle giant in August 1966, just before he joined the expansion Chicago Bulls. Bob scored 18 points per game that winter, including 40 on Christmas night at the old Madison Square Garden. She, too, experienced the glamour of America's biggest cities. The shopping! The food! But after the playoffs, Boozer asked his bride to think about their life after basketball. To put down roots in ... you guessed it.

Did Ella want to move to Omaha? "Noooooo."

Bob Boozer averaged 15 points and eight rebounds in 11 NBA seasons, but his best years came in Chicago.

But Boozer had a unique stature there. As racial conflict ripped his city apart, the 6-foot-8 power forward bridged two worlds. He made friends in the black barbershops of North 24th Street and in the white boardrooms downtown. He taught basketball clinics at Bryant Center and trained for management at Northwestern Bell Telephone Co.

He stewed over discrimination as much as anyone, but he didn't threaten violence. Politicians cozied up to him.

Boozer had another reason to come home. His 61-year-old mother was dying of cancer in the house where he grew up.

Viola Boozer lived at 25th and Erskine when Bob's father died in 1959. She lived there in '66 when fires burned and National Guardsmen marched within a block of her front door. "She wanted us to hurry up and move out of the ghetto," Ella said.

But Bob and Ella stayed with her in the spring of 1967. His favorite part of the old house was upstairs, which he remodeled as a mini-apartment. His new wife preferred the front porch, where they sat on spring nights and listened to Bob Gibson pitch on the radio. Sunday mornings they heard the organ and clapping across the street at Greater Bethlehem Temple.

In April, Bob celebrated his 30th birthday. When Mom died in May, it was time to move from 25th and Erskine.

He liked two houses, but real estate agents said no — those homes were "restricted by the owners." So the Boozers decided to build. They found a big lot in Colonial Acres, one of the tallest points in the city. Just up the hill from Forest Lawn Cemetery, where Bob buried his mother.

Bob Boozer frequently interacted with North Omaha kids in the offseason. Once he hired Omaha University's Marlin Briscoe to rebound for him. Even paid him. "And he's the cheapest man in the world," Briscoe said.

Eleven days after the funeral and 48 hours after Omaha's most bitter civil rights battle culminated in the State Capitol, they prepared to sign a contract.

That's when Boozer got a reminder that even a man his size can't straddle two worlds.

***

Three turbulent years earlier, a 26-year-old Creighton law student walked into the City Council chamber and injected levity into the opening rounds of a blood-boiling debate on open housing.

Ernie Chambers hadn't yet adopted his trademark cut-off sweatshirt, so he pinned the tag to his lapel: "Would you let your daughter marry a real estate man?"

Laughs were hard to find.

North Omaha busted at the concrete seams. In the early 1960s, an average of five black faces — mostly Southern and poor — arrived in the neighborhood every day.

Members of the Human Relations Board tour housing conditions at 1500 N. 20th in 1964.

The number of school-age black kids had doubled in 10 years. From 1960 to 1965, the overall black population jumped from 25,000 to 35,000. Almost all were confined to two square miles north of downtown, where most homes were built between 1880 and 1910. In 57 percent of houses, the number of residents exceeded the number of rooms.

Black homeowners couldn't get loans or insurance to fix roofs. Black renters paid exorbitant prices for dilapidated homes. "The single most profitable investment in Omaha today is the leasing of substandard housing," Mayor A.V. Sorensen said.

Slumlords wouldn't make basic repairs. Light bulbs hung from frayed cords. Wires poked out of walls. Broken pipes reeked of sewage. Windows and doors were missing.

In the early '60s, house fires killed 28 people in North Omaha. Federal aid to dependent children doubled. The black unemployment rate jumped into double digits. Police arrested one in five black kids before his 17th birthday, compared with one in 25 whites.

Politicians pushed for stricter enforcement of minimum housing standards and urban renewal, giving the government power to seize blighted land, buy it, clear it and resell it to private developers. Blacks resisted, worrying that such a plan would uproot them with no place to go.

The heart of the matter wasn't slum clearance, blacks said, it was housing segregation. According to one study, Omaha's racial divide equaled Birmingham, Alabama.

Enter the real estate agents, who frequently refused to show houses to black buyers in white neighborhoods. Or they abandoned deals fearing it might ruin their good names.

In 1963, real estate icon and former city councilman N.P. Dodge issued an extraordinary defense of his industry. Housing above all else, he wrote, exposes whites' fear of social integration.

> "I don't believe the Negro fully comprehends the depth of this feeling nor the distinction between this barrier and others, such as job opportunity and education.
>
> "The white man will trade and work with the Negro. He will purchase from a Negro clerk, ride in the same bus, eat in the same restaurant, occupy the same hotel. ...
>
> "This same average white family will not purchase a house next to a Negro's home and if a Negro family buys next to him, he will move.
>
> "No real estate agent can alone change the pattern. Wherever it has been tried, he risks bankruptcy because the 90 percent white majority on whom he depends for his livelihood will cease to trade with him. Any business which loses 90 percent of its customers fails. ...
>
> "When the white neighborhood will accept a Negro as a neighbor, as it is now doing on an increasingly broader scale in restaurants, stores, hotels and offices, this last barrier to first-class citizenship will disappear."

In April 1964, as Cassius Clay changed his name to Muhammad Ali, prompting a national backlash, Omaha blacks targeted the "last barrier." They wanted a local ordinance making it illegal for a homeowner or his agent to refuse to sell, rent or lease on the basis of race. Councilmen, fearing their own white backlash, preferred to let the voters decide. They delayed action over and over, including on April 28, 1964.

"For less cause than you are giving us here today, a revolution was waged," Chambers said. "You are telling me that America is incapable of granting full rights to every citizen. You think about that."

***

James Freeman came to Omaha in 1966 as one of the Omaha Public Schools' first black high school teachers. Like Ella Boozer, he didn't know what to expect.

The 23-year-old graduate of the Tuskegee Institute rode from the airport down 30th Street. When they turned onto Paxton Boulevard, Freeman asked his driver why there were so many "For Sale" signs. The answer: A black family had bought a house near there. Now other white owners raced to leave, too.

"That was my first memory of Omaha," Freeman recalled.

Once white flight started, agents exploited the fear factor to sell more houses. Many whites would have stayed if there were just a few black families on their street. But inevitably, one seller said, whites would become the minority.

James Freeman

Property Rights

"They have a right to a home just like anyone else," a white homeowner said. "But I hope the neighbors don't all sell to Negroes."

Across the city, blacks encountered the same problems. One bought a house in all-white Rockbrook — 3624 S. 94th St. When he hired a painter to change the color, his neighbor across the street ordered the man to leave.

The raised ranch was two different colors "until we could find a workman with enough backbone to finish the job," the owner later wrote.

His name? Bob Gibson.

"Why do you move out of the ghetto?" Gibson said in his autobiography. "Because it's the ghetto. I want the better things in life just like everybody else."

There was another motivation, though.

In 1965, Bob Rose — mentor to Marlin Briscoe and the Sayers brothers — moved his family to 5617 N. 63rd St., near Benson Golf Course. He wanted a nicer home. He also felt a responsibility to lead. To break out of the box so others could follow.

Rose took his family on long weekend drives through the country. They packed the car and headed to Nebraska City to pick apples.

Monday mornings Rose commuted back to the black neighborhood, where he taught at Horace Mann. He mentored Dick Davis and Johnny Rodgers. When they fell short, he extended his term of endearment, "sad sack." When they really messed up, he pulled out the strap.

His own son had it even harder. Bob Rose Jr. attended Nathan Hale, a white school just down the street from their new home. He learned patience and tolerance. He got a better education. But socially, he was always on alert. He frequently heard the N-word.

While classmates chased girls and passed notes, Bob Jr. kept his head down. He never asked to be a pioneer.

***

Ed Danner heard all the horror stories. He yearned to make a difference.

But as he walked into the State Capitol on Jan. 3, 1967 — the only black face in the 77th session of the Nebraska Legislature — Danner didn't seem equipped to represent the civil rights movement anymore.

He wasn't educated or brash like Ernie Chambers. He wasn't eloquent or radical like Stokely Carmichael. He was an old man in a young man's game.

State Sen. Edward Danner.

Born in 1900 in Guthrie, Oklahoma — the same county Marlin Briscoe's ancestors came from — Danner was 10 when his father died. He didn't graduate from high school.

Danner migrated to Omaha and butchered cattle at Swift before rising to vice president of the local packinghouse union. He raised nine kids on Pinkney Street and didn't miss Sundays at Zion Baptist, where he was a deacon.

In 1963, Danner entered the Legislature and made headlines when a Lincoln cafe refused to serve him. He sponsored his first open housing bill, gutting his own proposal when amendments rendered it worthless. In 1965, he tried open housing again, but it failed in committee.

Danner's activist constituents thought he was out of touch — they hated when he labeled them "Negro" instead of "black." They thought he yielded too much to the white establishment. They called him a "Tom."

But in 1967, the old butcher itched for a fight. He proposed open housing one more time. The governor supported Legislative Bill 358. So did business leaders and newspaper editorial boards. A full-page ad on page 9 of The World-Herald featured the names and addresses of 1,865 Omahans.

> The motto of the great State of Nebraska proclaims as a goal of our state "Equality before the law." Unfortunately, for many Nebraskans, equality is severely restricted — particularly when they look for a place to live.
>
> Racial discrimination in housing has ... been well documented as a major underlying cause of many social ills. It creates ghettos, which typically receive inferior education, health care, street improvements, law enforcement, and other public services. Discrimination divides the community, and destroys many of the individuals affected ...
>
> In this Centennial Year of the State of Nebraska, we hereby declare as our goal that these injustices, which have made a mockery of our state motto, shall be relegated to Nebraska's first century — that Nebraska celebrate its Centennial by enacting fair housing legislation with enforcement procedures to proclaim and assure "Equality before the law" to be a reality for all citizens.

The barrier still loomed large. Riots and demonstrations had increased white opposition to open housing across America. A year earlier, 51 percent of Americans opposed open housing. In 1967, it rose to 63 percent. Moreover, Danner's rivals in the Legislature came primarily from rural Nebraska. Their only images of North Omaha were stereotypes.

In May 1967, Danner had lunch with Scottsbluff maverick Terry Carpenter, a state senator also born in 1900. "Terrible Terry," as his constituents called him, earned a congressional seat during the Depression before failing nine times in bids for governor and the Senate. He started Nebraska's only gasoline refinery, became a millionaire and founded the village of Terrytown. He followed nobody.

If you can show me this ghetto exists, Carpenter told Danner, I might vote for open housing.

On May 23, the same day Bob Boozer's mother died, Danner stood before his legislative colleagues and wept, pleading with senators to delay judgment on his bill and join him on a tour of North Omaha.

State Sen. Edward Danner testifying for the open housing law, June 6 1967.

Let me show you.

One week later, 40 senators took a timeout from lawmaking, boarded an air-conditioned bus and embarked on a field trip. Imagine rolling up North 24th Street for the first time — like the Negro League buses in the 1940s — and seeing the best of North Omaha: Skeet's BBQ and Bryant Center, Goodwin's Barbershop and Kountze Park.

They saw the worst, too. Peeling paint and sagging roofs, junked-out cars in open lots and houses marked with yellow signs — "Condemned." Black faces stared at them curiously from front yards. For 90 minutes, senators looked out their bus windows but never stopped and got out.

Danner hoped the tour "opened some eyes." But his opponents left with a different observation.

"I saw a lot of very poor housing," said Sen. Lester Harsh of Bartley. "But I can take you to any small town and some farms and show you housing just as poor."

Carpenter's assessment was more damning: "The area wasn't as dilapidated as I was led to believe it is."

Danner felt a pang of regret: Maybe he was better off leaving North Omaha to their imaginations.

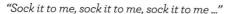

"R-E-S-P-E-C-T. Find out what it means to me ..."

On the morning of June 5, 1967, America's No. 1 song pumped through cars and cafes on 24th Street. At the Fair Deal, aka "Black City Hall," community leaders talked politics over eggs, grits and (if the conversation was good) a slice of sweet potato pie.

"R-E-S-P-E-C-T. Take care, TCB ..."

Halfway around the world, the Middle East erupted in a six-day war, a conflict that doubled Israel's territory and drew the battle lines for the next half-century. Overnight torrential rain left eastern Nebraska under water. But Aretha Franklin kept singing.

"Sock it to me, sock it to me, sock it to me ..."

State Sen. Terry Carpenter.

Down in Lincoln, North Omaha's elected voice walked into the Capitol for the defining debate of his career. And when Sen. Carpenter motioned to dismiss LB 358, Ed Danner spoke up.

He cited support from Nelson Rockefeller and Robert McNamara. He pointed to open housing laws in 23 states, including Colorado, where real estate agents fought legislation until realizing it actually benefited their business.

Danner referenced studies showing that desegregated housing lessened prejudice because it improved black/white communication. He picked apart the notion that government can't regulate private property. What about eminent domain, zoning and construction codes? Without an open housing law, Danner said, "those advocating Black Power retain one of their most powerful weapons." Then Danner ceded the floor to Sen. William Swanson, a Lincoln real estate agent.

"I'm certain that no thinking member of this Legislature can deny that a problem exists. Most of us last week saw it firsthand — living conditions in parts of Omaha which are deplorable. ... Discrimination and inequality are and must be a burden on our social conscience. ...

"But let's reduce LB 358 to a matter of economics for a moment. Let's suppose that a retired couple invested their life savings in a 10- or 12-unit apartment house. ... If this couple advertises an apartment for rent, they cannot refuse to rent to anyone on certain designated grounds. Suppose for a moment that these owners do rent to a member of a minority group. What happens? Too often the other tenants move out and vacancies are almost impossible to fill. In the rent business, vacancies kill you off and the apartment house becomes a white elephant. ...

"Now what's wrong with this situation? I'll tell you what's wrong. This bill says it's unlawful for the owner to discriminate even though it may lead to his financial ruin. The real culprits are the other tenants who move out."

Danner had tried to persuade through empirical evidence. Now the old butcher, frequently mocked by black youths because he wasn't articulate or educated, delivered an argument that Ernie Chambers would have endorsed.

Property Rights

"I'd like to remind you again that the bullets on the battlefield do not discriminate. ... The burden that the soldier on the battlefield bears — the Negro soldier bears — is just as heavy as the pack that the white soldier bears, but the Negro soldier at home bears a far heavier burden because he is denied the right of rental of property. He's all right to give his life, fight for the government, defend the nation, but you can't live in certain places. ...

"I have a son that spent 15 years of his life in the Air Force. ... His mother received a call the other day that he is going to have to go to Vietnam. ... You're saying because of the pigment of his skin being dark, he doesn't have a right to live in rental property?"

There must have been part of Danner that believed he'd won right there. That undecided senators would rally behind him, like in a Hollywood movie. Instead, Sen. Herbert Nore of Genoa took the floor and began reading a letter he'd received.

"The people who live in these slum areas have no one to blame but themselves. If they would get off the corner bar stool and use the money that they spend on drinks for some paint and paper and such, their homes would be livable. Instead of driving big expensive automobiles they would get a cheaper one and put food on the table and clothing on their backs. ... They have made their own ghettos and are now wanting for the government to furnish them with new homes, food, and clothing so they can have more money for luxuries."

Sen. Clifton Batchelder threw the next verbal punch. An Omaha resident, Batchelder once sat on the Near North YMCA board. Now he led the charge against open housing, citing British statesman William Pitt's 18th-century speech before the House of Lords:

"Although the peasant's house is made of thatch and the wind and the snow may enter, the king and all his legions may not."

The "repulsive" open housing proposal, Batchelder said, weakened "the most greatly cherished right that Americans have."

"I would think that the members of the minority groups would realize that this is not good salesmanship to push this. They need the friendship. They need the cooperation. They need the respect of all of these people and yet they are so impatient. ...

"The conditions that they describe ... have been exaggerated. The amount that will be accomplished by the passage of this law has been exaggerated. Their own progress has been minimized. Also, they have exaggerated the good for their cause that will come from the passage of this law."

Sen. Carpenter, the old titan of the Legislature, waited to throw the knockout blow. He didn't bother with housing.

"When I heard men like Carmichael on television ... advocate the insurrection and the destruction of this form of government and when I see them surrounded by the Black Panthers and the other people such as Cassius Clay ... I don't care how bad the situation is. White or black. No man has a right to advocate the destruction of this government. We have Cassius Clay, a man of great faith. He's willing to tear the head off of every one of his opponents, but in order to shirk his responsibility as a good citizen he says he's a minister. If he's a minister, I'm a monkey's uncle."

A cold shoulder

If Bob Gibson had played for the Chicago Cubs, New York Yankees or Los Angeles Dodgers, he might have left Omaha for good. But in the early 1960s, blacks in St. Louis faced a housing market even more segregated than Omaha's. "I couldn't find a place to live," Gibson said. "Not the kind of place that I wanted."

Gibson's hometown wasn't much better, but at least he had family there. So he returned to Omaha every offseason.

After his 3763 Maple St. house burned in May 1966, his first wife, Charline, found one she liked in west Omaha — Rockbrook. Gibson came home after the season and had to stop at a payphone to ask Charline where it was.

"Nice house," he said upon arrival.

It came with a catch. Multiple neighbors didn't want to live next to a black family, even the '64 World Series MVP.

They eventually came around. One helped decorate Gibson's house following the '67 Series. Another approached Gibson in tears, apologizing for his behavior. "He realized what an ass he was," Gibson said in an interview.

Bob Gibson's kids and neighbors decorate his home after his Game 7 World Series win in 1967.

Above, Gibson with his daughter Annette.

Gibson's daughter became friends with the man's son. Bob even invited the man over for Christmas parties. But he refused to go inside that neighbor's house.

"Did I forgive him? Yeah. But I didn't forget. I still haven't forgotten."

Danner didn't let the remark slide.

"If all the white people exemplify bigotry as this senator does, then I can understand why Mr. Carmichael thinks as he does," Danner said. "It's this kind of thing that has been going on for 100 years. This same thing we find here today."

But Danner's sense of history and injustice reached deeper than 1865.

During debate, he spoke of his Vietnam-bound son who couldn't rent an apartment. Danner didn't reference a character just as relevant to the discussion — his father.

When Sen. Batchelder declared that "the hellish part of this whole situation" is the erosion of a right that "has come to us so torturously over so many years down through so many ages," he certainly wasn't describing the experience of a man like Mack Danner.

Born in Mississippi in 1859, two years before the South fought a war to preserve slavery, Ed's father didn't have a right to property.

He *was* property.

The following morning, June 6, 1967, senators cast their final votes — 28-21 — to kill open housing again. Danner walked out of the chamber and informed the sergeant-at-arms he wouldn't be there for the next order of business: the Legislature's official portrait for 1967. Centennial edition.

The photograph shows 48 white senators and one empty desk.

***

Boozer addresses the media in June 1967.

Two days later, Bob Boozer got a phone call from his housing developer: The deal was off.

Emboldened by the legislative vote, 30 percent of homeowners in Colonial Acres "strongly objected" to a black man moving to their hill. They threatened to "wreck" the development if Boozer bought a lot.

"How do they have the right to sit on their fat mortgages and dictate whether I can move into this neighborhood?" said Boozer, whose annual NBA salary exceeded the cost of new construction. "If I could become white overnight, any community in Omaha would welcome me with open arms."

Boozer had scheduled two weeks of basketball clinics that summer at Bryant Center. When kids see a public figure treated unfairly, he said, "it sabotages all I'm trying to do and drives them into the arms of Stokely Carmichaels."

Passions burned hot in the summer of 1967. In San Francisco, hippies descended on Haight-Ashbury for the Summer of Love. In Houston, a jury convicted Muhammad Ali for refusing induction in the armed forces. In urban ghettoes across the country, race riots flared in the streets. Omaha remained relatively cool.

Downtown cranes constructed the city's first skyscraper, the Woodmen Tower. Nebraska changed its license plate from "Beef State" to "Cornhusker State".

In September, a healthy Marlin Briscoe returned to All-American form at Omaha University, escaping the pocket, scrambling around defenses, firing lasers downfield.

"Every time he'd make a throw," teammate Lew Garrison said, "you'd say, how did he do that?"

"What sets him off from all the other players I've coached is his basic instinct of sensing people around him," coach Al Caniglia said. "At times he almost seemed to have radar."

Briscoe's tricks earned him a nickname: The Magician.

In October, Gibson returned from a broken leg suffered in midseason and won three more World Series games, including Game 7 at Fenway Park. In 27 innings against the Red Sox, Gibson recorded 26 strikeouts and yielded just three runs.

Six days before Christmas 1967, the sports heroes of North Omaha gathered at the Wesley House for the Super-Star Banquet. Bob Devaney attended. His assistant Monte Kiffin spoke.

Deacon Jones (left), Monte Kiffin, Bob Boozer and Roger Sayers at the Wesley House sports banquet, Dec. 19, 1967.

Boozer flew in from Chicago, where Wilt Chamberlain had just outscored him in one game 68-27. Boozer and Gibson described how Josh Gibson groomed them to be great with frequent kicks in the butt. Roger Sayers told stories of Bob Rose motivating Gale when he was just an 85-pound eighth-grader.

The night felt like a reunion. It might have been the calm before the storm. A week later, North Omaha flipped the calendar to the year that — for better or worse — defined their generation and the neighborhood.

1968.

Chapter 8

Losing their Rhythm

WHEN THE MOVIE ENDED, the real show began.

The bearded black barber in a tight white T-shirt stepped to the podium and addressed a packed dining hall on the University of Nebraska-Lincoln campus. Ernie Chambers wasted no time.

He called Christians hypocrites. Attacked Omaha Public Schools for physically abusing black students. Blasted politicians for corruption and indifference. While white UNL students sit in class and wonder about their next date, Chambers said, blacks worry about their families.

"Negroes have been put in a position with no alternative but to fight back," Chambers said. "I am for fighting back."

It was Monday night, Feb. 5, 1968. Halfway around the world, the Viet Cong attacked Army and Marine battalions in the ancient capital of Hue. Saigon streets crackled with machine-gun fire. The Tet Offensive, a series of bloody attacks on South Vietnam, entered its second week.

In Lincoln that day, Southeast High School named 23-year-old Frank Solich its new football coach. And that night, a few hundred UNL students squeezed into the Selleck dining hall to watch "A Time for Burning."

In 1968 Ernie Chambers told UNL students to confront their prejudice.

The Oscar-nominated documentary featured an Omaha pastor's attempt to build bridges between his all-white church, Augustana Lutheran, and the black community. Rev. William Youngdahl's movement failed and his church forced his resignation. One of the opening scenes captured Chambers in his Spencer Street barbershop lecturing the pastor.

> *"I can't solve the problem. You guys pull the strings that close schools. You guys throw the bombs that keep our kids restricted to the ghetto. You guys write up the restrictive covenants that keep us out of houses. So it's up to you to talk to your brothers and your sisters and persuade them that they have a responsibility. We've assumed ours for over 400 years. And we're tired of this kind of stuff now.'"*

When the lights turned on at Selleck, Chambers engaged a diverse audience, challenging white college kids to confront their prejudice. Some cheered him. Some mocked him.

"This is just a lark, a show for you," the 30-year-old Chambers said, "but it gives me a chance to show how little I think of you."

Down the hall, a 30-year-old white assistant football coach supervised athletic study hall. Tom Osborne was in charge of academics, monitoring GPAs and making sure 150 football players passed 24 credit hours.

"It was an uncomfortable position," Osborne recalled. "I was the one guy and I was always dreading that somehow I would mess up and I'd have to go see Bob Devaney and tell him one of his best players was ineligible."

At about 9 p.m., Osborne headed out through the dining hall and saw the congregation. He intended to keep walking until he heard the man up front criticize Devaney for the way he handled black players, dozens of whom were listening.

Osborne stopped.

"It just caught me by surprise. Some of the things I was hearing didn't square with my observation. ... If there was anybody who didn't have a prejudiced bone in his body, it was Bob Devaney."

Osborne raised his hand and spoke up. And Chambers didn't back down. "They got into it," said Mike Green, former Husker running back.

Nebraska assistant Tom Osborne, right, and head coach Bob Devaney in 1969.

Then Green's buddy got pulled into the fray. Dick Davis, a 1965 North High grad, had helped reverse the trend of North Omaha blacks rejecting the Huskers. Ernie cut Davis' hair, but Dick had no beef with Nebraska. That same month, Devaney had helped Davis' fiancée get an apartment after discrimination undercut her application.

So Osborne called on Davis to share his experience. To Chambers, that was putting a young black player on the spot. *Leave him out of this.* In the end, Davis said nothing.

Over the next 50 years, two of the most influential men in Nebraska history — as different as the hair on their heads — argued publicly about all kinds of issues, from Jarvis Redwine's demotion (1980) to student-athlete stipends (1985). In 1993, they debated pornography laws. Chambers asked Osborne if he'd ever seen the Sports Illustrated swimsuit issue. "Before I quit reading Sports Illustrated, yes," Osborne said.

As they aged, they became more cordial. But that night at Selleck? Not so much. Their exchange foreshadowed the bigger conflicts of 1968, when people — black and white — stood up and declared what they believed, consequences be damned. And every once in a while, a black athlete found himself in the middle of the madness.

"That was the first time I'd ever seen Ernie," Osborne said. "Didn't even know who he was."

The football coach listened a few more minutes, then headed out into the quiet winter night. A more hostile foe was coming Chambers' way.

***

George Wallace stepped off his private plane to the soothing notes of "Dixie." If the band had been all he heard, the former Alabama governor might have felt welcome. He wasn't.

"Wallace, Go Home!"

"Sock it to me, Black Power!"

How many men could've attracted 1,500 people to Eppley Airfield on Sunday afternoon, March 3, 1968? Muhammad Ali? Doubtful. The Beatles? Maybe. But few inspired such love and loathing as America's chief spokesman for segregation.

As Wallace shook hands with his fans, protesters chanted "We shall overcome." A foe heaved at him a partly burned Confederate flag — it missed. Inside the terminal, Wallace — a mere 5-foot-7 — addressed the media, promising to take guns from bad guys and give them to good guys; shift the tax burden from the poor to the rich; repeal open housing laws; and win Vietnam by freeing generals to fight. He denied he was racist.

Wallace supporters welcome him at Eppley Airfield.

Presidential candidate George Wallace arrives in Omaha, March 3, 1968.

"You have had more lack of tranquility in your own state than we have had in our state," Wallace said.

There was enough anger to go around. That same week, "CBS Evening News" anchor Walter Cronkite closed his Vietnam report with a declaration that America should give up the fight and come home.

The bipartisan Kerner Commission released its much-anticipated report examining the causes of the 1967 urban riots. The report, immediately controversial, focused its critique on the majority.

"What white Americans have never fully understood but what the Negro can never forget — is that white society is deeply implicated in the ghetto," the commission concluded. "White institutions created it, white institutions maintain it, and white society condones it."

North Omahans didn't have time to argue about 1967. They focused on the '68 presidential election.

In mid-February, Wallace's Nebraska supporters launched a third political party to put him on the May 14 presidential primary ballot. To get the required 750 signatures, Wallace scheduled a March 4 speech at the Civic Auditorium, less than a mile from North Omaha's front door.

"Can you imagine how we felt as black folks?" activist Rodney Wead said.

A showdown loomed. But first Wallace paid a visit to the University of Nebraska at Omaha, where a few hundred students (mostly opponents) met him in the parking lot with signs: "Burn Bigot Burn," "Let me go to jail and Wallace go to hell," "When will the Civil War end?"

Wallace spoke to a political science class for 30 minutes as police officers kept protesters at bay.

"The average man is sick and tired of people who talk about free speech, but don't want you to speak," he said. "If I were president ... and some anarchist lies down in front of my automobile, it will be the last automobile he ever lies down in front of."

Professor Richard Marvel's students shared Wallace's version of the truth: that America had lost its way not because it was changing too slowly, but too fast. They responded with a sound you don't often hear in a college classroom.

Cheers.

***

Four miles east, on the hill overlooking downtown, Nebraska's best high school basketball team prepared for a state championship run. Omaha Central rolled through winter with just one loss, captivating crowds and inspiring a nickname from The World-Herald's Don Lee.

"The Rhythm Boys."

"We were the talk of the town," Willie Frazier said.

Central's first all-black starting lineup honed its game at Bryant Center, the Boys Club and Kountze Park. The Eagles could dribble, pass and shoot, but what made them special was their anchor, a 6-foot-7 free spirit.

Dwaine Dillard.

On Feb. 16, 1968, No. 1 Central hosted No. 2 Creighton Prep at Norris Junior High. The gym reached 3,200 capacity almost two hours before the 8 p.m. tip. Central "bombed Creighton Prep out of sight," The World-Herald's Paul LeBar wrote, thanks mainly to Dillard's dominance.

The big guy averaged 23 points and 21 boards, his numbers frequently leaping off the sports page:

• 34 points, 30 rebounds, 10 blocks and four steals against Council Bluffs Abraham Lincoln.

• 32 points and 25 rebounds against Bryan.

Dillard blocked shots, LeBar wrote, "as if he were swatting flies."

Dwaine Dillard No. 14 with Central teammate John Biddle No. 22.

"No one could stop him," former Central teammate Alvin Mitchell said.

Except distractions.

Dillard was born to a 16-year-old student at South High. His father went off to the Army and eventually left the picture. Dillard bounced from city to city, including a short stint as a foster child, before spending most of grade school next to Marlin Briscoe in the South Omaha projects.

In high school, his grandma — a Swift packinghouse worker — moved him to North Omaha, 24th and Sprague. Dillard, often the class clown, made fast friends (and girl-friends) with a magnetic personality. He could spring into a handstand and walk around the gym upside down.

Losing their Rhythm

Central Coach Warren Marquiss, standing, talks with his 1968 team after practice.

"You don't see many 6-7 guys doing that," Central assistant Jim Martin said.

Dillard found mischief everywhere. At his most innocent, he piggybacked on a 5-7 teammate, ripped his hand open dunking in pre-game warmups, sneaked out of a bowling alley without paying for his food — sticking his buddies with the bill — and drowned his stomach with sugar.

One day before practice, Dillard came walking down the hallway drinking from a paper cup.

Free Pepsi, he said. Dillard and his teammates emptied the fountain pop machine, only to find out it was intended for a parents event.

"You guys have really done it," his coach said.

Dillard's antics weren't always harmless. By star athlete standards, he spent too much time smoking, drinking and gambling in South Omaha pool halls. During the 1966 unrest, police arrested him for breaking into a TV repair shop and department store — charges were dropped.

"Dwaine was always doing something," Mitchell said.

Wallace protesters make their voices heard in the Civic Auditorium's balcony on March 4, 1968.

***

The Eagles finished Monday afternoon basketball practice as the sun set over their century-old high school. A beautiful 65-degree night.

One block down the hill, protesters arrived in front of the Civic Auditorium for the Wallace speech, carrying signs like "White Fascism" and "Wallaceness is Lawlessness." They ranged from black teens to white priests and nuns.

Organizers ushered most of the 500 protesters to the balcony. But police officers led a group of about 20 — mostly young and black — to the best seats in the house, the arena floor right in front of the podium. A strategic move by Wallace, Nebraska Gov. Norbert Tiemann later said.

The Civic Auditorium's northern half was closed off by curtains, leaving 5,400 people for 3,400 seats — 2,400 in the balcony and 1,000 on the floor. The atmosphere felt like a prize fight — cramped, hot and hostile. Protesters punctuated the Pledge of Allegiance with shouts — "With liberty and justice for all!" During the national anthem, stink bombs filled the auditorium.

Wallace backers, many of whom wore straw hats, passed plastic buckets like church offering plates, collecting cash for the campaign. Wallace protesters cut the cables from the platform to TV cameras. They heckled speakers.

"Every catcall," said the Rev. Henry Bucklew, a Wallace ally from Mississippi, "is worth 10 signatures for Governor Wallace."

When the candidate finally came to the microphone after 9 p.m., protesters in front of the podium — now 40-50 — shouted over him, throwing signs and sticks.

"These are the kind of folks the people in this country are sick and tired of," Wallace shouted. He spoke for about 10 minutes before police closed in on the protesters. That's when tensions exploded.

According to multiple accounts, a white officer and a black protester exchanged words. The cop knocked him down and when the teenager attempted to retaliate, police swarmed the demonstrators with billy clubs and mace.

Flying fists, flailing clubs and fleeing demonstrators during the Wallace convention.

Rodney Wead and fellow demonstrators attempt to re-enter the Civic Auditorium.

"They kicked my butt," said Wead, who still wears a scar near his eye 50 years later.

Some fought back, others turned and tried to escape down a long center aisle — a gantlet in enemy territory. Wallace supporters swung folding chairs. One officer hit a young black man as a Wallace supporter held him. Two white men kicked a black girl. Violence spilled into the street, where protesters busted car windshields.

Within five minutes, the arena calmed and Wallace continued his 45-minute speech.

"My prayer tonight is that God bless all people — black and white — and that our system, under attack by those with not many votes but an abundance of influence, be saved."

When he finished, Wallace got a standing ovation and more than 2,000 signatures — his third party was official. The Rev. Bucklew: "Nebraska places the name of George C. Wallace on the ballot. ... Never before in any state or city has success come any quicker. No longer can Alabama claim George Wallace. He belongs to America."

Wallace hurried out to a waiting car, leaving behind a night of mayhem.

"Why?" a black teenager said in the auditorium lobby, sobbing. "Why?!" she screamed at a policeman. "Why?" she said to a black man holding a handkerchief to a gash on his head.

Then the girl saw a group of white people passing by and spat at their feet.

***

Protesters retreated up North 24th Street and by 10:30 p.m., about 200 people gathered at 24th and Lake. They threw rocks and bottles at cars and storefront windows, targeting white-owned businesses.

When an 18-year-old white man stopped at the traffic light, a rioter heaved a brick at his head, putting the stranger in the hospital. A group of young blacks pulled a 52-year-old white man from his pickup truck and beat him into critical condition.

Police reinforced their ranks. At 12:15 a.m., a 23-year-old off-duty officer, who worked the Wallace convention downtown, responded to a radio call at Crosstown Loan and Pawn, where rioters had broken the front window and torn apart the security bars.

James Abbott entered the pawn shop with his 12-gauge riot gun — prohibited for an off-duty officer — and waited in the dark. Just before 3 a.m., 16-year-old Howard Stevenson crawled through a broken window and, according to the officer, began opening a sliding-glass door for other intruders.

From 33 feet, Abbott pulled the trigger. The bullet nearly ripped Stevenson's body in half.

Anger didn't end at sunrise. Thousands of OPS students skipped Tuesday classes after erroneous reports that schools were closed. Those who did attend didn't stay long.

At Horace Mann Junior High — 97 percent black — students staged a walkout at 10:04 a.m, gathering on the Kountze Park basketball courts, where their heroes played pickup games. A few middle schoolers broke more than 50 windows and set ablaze two bushes.

Horace Mann students staged a walkout the morning after George Wallace's speech.

Who showed up to keep the peace? The most militant black man of all, Ernie Chambers.

"How in the world are people like me going to help you if you do something like this?" he told the crowd as windows shattered behind him.

Chambers pointed to TV cameras recording the scene.

"You are putting on a show for the crackers. They are going to make it look like you are a bunch of thugs. Don't let them make a show out of you."

In the 72 hours after George Wallace, North Omaha didn't burn like it did in July 1966. The National Guard didn't march down 24th Street at 1 a.m. So why did the 1968 disturbances set off such a panic? Because of what happened in broad daylight, specifically in schools.

A Molotov cocktail exploded in a North High hallway. Tech students threw rocks at Cuming Street traffic. Central students engaged in fights and walkouts. Horace Mann students tried to break into Lothrop and Saratoga Schools during classes.

Absentees exceeded 60 percent at Tech, Central and North the rest of the week. Panic gripped white suburban students who worried that blacks might attack — many families left the city until tensions cooled. Ten white mothers visited the Mayor's Office demanding more security at North High. "We want protection and until we get it our children aren't going back to school."

After three days of unrest, police disperse youths gathered at 36th and Boyd, March 7, 1968.

On streets, blacks attacked whites with pop bottles, tire irons and razors. Two blocks east of North High — at 2:30 p.m. — a 15-year-old white girl brandished a shotgun and charged at 30 blacks. Her sister stepped in and stopped a potential massacre.

Gun sales in early March tripled from the year before. J.C. Penney alone sold 255 more rifles and shotguns that week. Pistol registrations quadrupled. When a new Kmart store opened at 71st and Ames, 10 handguns sold in the first few hours. "Customers weren't buying them for target practice," a spokesman said.

Mayor Sorensen, the man who defended blacks during the 1966 riot, even lecturing U.S. senators in Washington about conditions in the ghetto, switched sides.

He blistered protesters for harassing "Mr. Wallace." He defended officers' "superb" response at the Civic. He criticized the Kerner Commission, blaming "a very small group of minority citizens who apparently feel that progress will come through the type of antagonism reflected at the Auditorium."

The protests angered Omahans. "Many people are truly disturbed and I confess I am one of them," Sorensen said.

Gov. Tiemann had a different take on Wallace, saying his visit was "like throwing gasoline on a fire." Wallace set the stage for a confrontation. Police should've put all demonstrators in the balcony or escorted them out before Wallace took the mic, he said. Tiemann prompted swift backlash from constituents when he called Wallace "that nut from Alabama."

By week's end, the damage included 44 cars, 32 buildings, 17 injuries and 55 arrests, including the Rev. John McCaslin of Holy Family Church, a white priest who advocated Black Power.

"There was a real thin line between right and wrong," Alvin Mitchell said.

But one teenager became the face of the 1968 disturbances — forever synonymous with George Wallace.

Late Tuesday night, 26 hours after Wallace fled Omaha, three white police officers stopped a car at 19th and Sprague and arrested six black men — ages 16-26 — for possession of flammable liquid-filled bottles. Molotov cocktails.

Dwaine Dillard was in the front seat.

Crosstown Loan Co., 1819 N. 24th Street, hours after an off-duty officer shot and killed Howard Stevenson. The 16-year-old entered the vandalized pawn shop through a broken window.

***

The flame flickered inside for a long time before that night.

High school standouts Johnny Rodgers and Ernie Britt had little interest in politics or protests. But Dillard was more socially conscious. Certainly more rebellious. Like Bill Russell and Muhammad Ali, he seemed to believe that black athletes could (and should) champion the cause of black freedom.

"We were chasing girls," Rodgers said. "He was chasing civil rights. And girls."

When Dillard listened to Ernie Chambers' speeches, he felt inspiration and anger. Maybe he felt invincible, too.

The night of Wallace's convention, Dillard occupied the street outside the Civic Auditorium. The next day, standing in a Central High stairwell landing, he lit a match and dropped it in a trash can. He threw a hamburger bun at a music instructor before walking out of class. He joined an after-school fistfight when he should've been lacing up for practice.

Tuesday night, March 5, Dillard played basketball at Bryant Center until 11 p.m., as he often did. His buddies, including Rodgers and Britt, headed home — the state tournament was 48 hours away.

But Dillard got in Nathaniel Goodwin's '66 blue Rambler. An hour later, he saw the flashing lights. His mom and minister picked him up Wednesday morning from police headquarters. Chambers was there, too, vowing to keep Dillard in line.

His face appeared on the front page of the Wednesday afternoon World-Herald. Local newscasts featured his arrest. Even Cronkite covered the unrest.

Dillard said he was just getting a ride home. His friends said the police lied about the explosives and roughed them up. But he'd lost control of his reputation — and his version of the truth. As World-Herald sports columnist Wally Provost wrote:

> "Dillard was not just another boy in trouble. He was a Symbol. To some people he was an accused criminal who should be dealt with firmly and promptly. He symbolized all that they feared from lawlessness. To another faction he was a school athletic hero, perhaps even an idolized rebel. Considering the extreme emotions of the city, this was a hot one; anybody who touched it could expect to get burned."

As Dillard stirred public debate, Mayor Sorensen stewed over the next big event at the Civic Auditorium: the Class A boys basketball state tournament. It had moved from Lincoln to Omaha in 1965. But Sorensen feared that returning to the source of unrest would invite more protests and more violence.

The Nebraska School Activities Association agreed and moved Class A to Lincoln. Central would play Thursday at 9:30 a.m. to minimize chances of violence.

Would the state's best player be in uniform? Coach Warren Marquiss, in his last season before retirement and his last chance to win Central's first state championship since 1912, argued that Dillard should be eligible — you can't punish a student before a fair trial. The superintendent and principal deferred to his judgment.

The decision to let Dillard play didn't satisfy angry strangers who called Marquiss' home so often that the coach disconnected his phone.

Wednesday night, as he should've been completing his game plan, Marquiss looked out his window at 2802 N. 69th St. and saw an image straight out of Alabama: two homemade crosses burning in the front yard.

Water extinguished the flames. The grass wore the scars.

***

Central was in good spirits when it reached Pershing Auditorium, despite a defection.

One of Dillard's teammates quit the team that morning, refusing to travel to Lincoln. His own personal protest against Wallace and the tournament move. Then Marquiss announced that Dillard would miss the opener. He had violated a team rule, the coach said.

The Eagles strongly considered a boycott. In the locker room, they actually voted not to play before Marquiss called their bluff. "Get out there!"

The State Patrol and Lincoln police were on riot alert. More than a dozen helmeted policemen, including a dog, ringed the courts at Pershing Auditorium and the NU Coliseum, where Tech played simultaneously. More officers stood high in the bleachers.

After riots broke out in Omaha, officials decided to move the state tournament to Lincoln. The State Patrol and Lincoln police were on alert, including at the Tech-Northeast game.

Central coach Warren Marquiss, left, Dwaine Dillard and team at the 1968 state basketball tournament.

They had a quiet morning. Only 1,000 fans showed up, few of them black. Central rolled North Platte, 70-51.

Dillard returned for the Friday morning semifinal against Boys Town, recording 23 points, 21 rebounds and four blocks in a 51-47 overtime win. At the NU Coliseum, Tech lost to Lincoln Northeast and Ernie Britt lost his cool, shoving an official after his fifth foul. Bob Devaney came out of the stands to calm him down.

Saturday morning presented a state championship rematch — Northeast beat Central in 1967. About 7,000 fans squeezed into the Coliseum, crowding the floor so tightly that officials allowed players to straddle the boundaries when inbounding the ball.

Pressure squeezed shooters, too. Central scored just 19 first-half points, but held a one-point lead. Then Northeast got hot. Dillard's 22 points and 17 rebounds couldn't overcome Central's 10-for-20 at the foul line. The Rhythm Boys never found their rhythm.

Lincoln Northeast 54, Omaha Central 50.

Dillard's big finale wasn't enough to win the championship.

Marquiss blamed five days of chaos. "We were emotionally drained." Dillard, on his 19th birthday, handled defeat with class. But neither Central nor North Omaha inspired sympathy.

In Sunday's Journal Star, Lincoln columnist Hal Brown wrote this: "If the Omaha Negroes responsible for the Monday night troubles in their city had been able to show the restraint under stress that was shown by the Central Negro cagers, the Class A competition would have been played in Omaha Saturday night instead of in Lincoln Saturday morning."

Here's the other way to look at it: What if Wallace hadn't come at all?

He never returned to Nebraska and received only 1 percent of votes in the May primary.

Police exonerated James Abbott, the cop who killed Howard Stevenson inside Crosstown Loan. Coincidentally, the two had attended the mayor's 1966 youth camp, designed to improve relationships between police and black youth.

Nathaniel Goodwin, the driver of the '66 Rambler, was convicted of possession of an explosive and sentenced to 1-3 years in jail. McCaslin left his position as director of the Catholic Social Action Office, but continued preaching.

And Dillard? Just like 1966, his charge was dropped. But he wore the scars. Scholarship opportunities dwindled. He landed at Eastern Michigan for one year, then returned to Omaha and never played college basketball again.

The Baltimore Bullets saw his potential and drafted him in the fifth round in 1972. It didn't work out. He joined the Washington Generals before earning a one-year promotion to the Harlem Globetrotters. He played three ABA games with the Utah Stars. But he never found a home in basketball. Like Fred Hare, Dillard carried the burden of "what if" the rest of his life.

"He was so bitter about basketball," his wife, Carolee, told author Steve Marantz in his book about the '68 Eagles, "The Rhythm Boys of Omaha Central."

Dwaine Dillard in an all-star game jersey in August 1968.

"He didn't want to talk much about it. He thought he should have gone further."

In 2008, Dillard died of pancreatic cancer. He was 59. His name still carries weight in the North Omaha barbershops and cafes. But the lessons are still fuzzy.

Alvin Mitchell, Dillard's old teammate and North Omaha pastor, reflects on a moment when moral compasses spun so fast you couldn't see straight, when the pressure to stand and shout felt overwhelming, when kids didn't see a future past the present. In the midst of chaos, Mitchell said, you have to stop and ask yourself, "Who will lead me?"

In March 1968, that question strained even the strongest coaches, politicians, ministers, cops and civil rights leaders.

For an 18-year-old basketball star, the line between right and wrong all but disappeared.

Chapter 9

Red-hot Summer

THE RIFLE BLAST SUCKED the air from the sky.

Not just in Memphis, where sirens surrounded the Lorraine Motel, but hundreds of miles away in Omaha. Marlin Briscoe finished a math class at UNO, one of the last impediments to his degree. He walked to the parking lot, climbed into his gray Buick Riviera and heard the radio report.

"I started crying," Briscoe recalled. "It was like somebody stabbed me in the heart."

Martin Luther King Jr. died that night, April 4, 1968, the victim of a white man's single rifle bullet. He was 39.

Since emerging as the face of civil rights a decade earlier, King's non-violent principles had lost favor with progressive blacks.

"As more militant Negroes cried 'Burn, Baby, Burn,'" an

Two days after Martin Luther King Jr.'s assassination, Valerie Ratles read a King speech in eulogy at North Omaha's Wesley House.

Omaha Star column explained, "King's strongest admirers questioned whether he could draw as large a crowd at his own alma mater as Stokely Carmichael, and sadly admitted that some students would boo him."

But no black man in America inspired as much respect and admiration. King's death, Ernie Chambers said hours after the blast, "could very well be the first shot of a civil war."

Riots erupted in Washington, D.C., Boston, Philly, Chicago, Detroit, Los Angeles, even Des Moines. But in North Omaha, exactly one month after the George Wallace unrest, blacks simply wept.

On April 7, about 2,000 people marched one mile from 24th Street to Salem Baptist Church for a memorial service. Hundreds more watched from cars, sidewalks and store windows. Kids led the way, holding up American flags and beating drums. Fathers in black armbands carried toddlers on their shoulders.

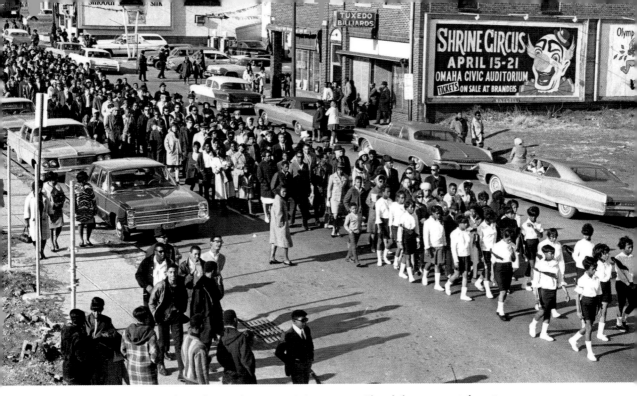

MLK mourners march south on 24th Street to Salem Baptist Church for a memorial service.

The church filled quickly and the crowd spilled into the street. State Sen. Ed Danner addressed an audience bigger than his neighborhood:

"America, I'm not sure God isn't going to make you pay. ... If you take a life of a man like Dr. King, what chance does Sen. Danner have?"

Major League Baseball postponed Opening Day for King's funeral in downtown Atlanta. The next night in St. Louis, reigning World Series MVP Bob Gibson recorded his first outs of 1968, arguably the greatest individual pitching season in baseball history.

Since 1919, only Gibson has recorded a single-season ERA lower than 1.52. He shattered the mark in '68 with a 1.12, thanks largely to an eight-week summer span that still defies logic. Ten starts, 10 complete games, 10 wins. And just two runs allowed.

But the numbers alone don't tell the story. During a time of deep racial and cultural conflict, Gibson embodied a character — an archetype — that white America didn't understand.

The angry black man.

1968 cranked those hostilities to a boiling point, especially back home. As the kid from the Logan Fontenelle projects became the most invincible force in sports, the ingredients that produced North Omaha's generation of athletes melted away.

One day after Dr. King's funeral, Gibson didn't give up an earned run in seven innings against the Braves.

The Cardinals were 1-0.

***

LBJ was out.

Four days before King's assassination, the president, weakened by Vietnam, stunned Americans with an Oval Office address: He wouldn't run for reelection in 1968.

His exit opened the door for two Democratic senators, Eugene McCarthy and Robert Kennedy. It also drew attention to Nebraska, one of only 14 states holding a primary. Kennedy and McCarthy opened campaign offices nine blocks apart on North 24th Street, within shouting distance of the next controversy.

On April 27, John Beasley was walking home from McCarthy's headquarters when he saw flashing lights at 24th and Franklin.

The 24-year-old followed the commotion behind a liquor store, where four cops had a black man in handcuffs on the ground while a fifth officer sprayed Mace in his face.

"What the hell are you doing?" Beasley recalls saying. "You already got him."

Rodney Wead discusses civil rights in April 1968.

Two of the officers had a reputation for harassing blacks. As a crowd of Logan Fontenelle residents gathered to protest, officers fired two shots in the air, warning the crowd to back away. One pointed a gun at Beasley's brother.

"Ten years ago, police could have used any method of breaking up a dice game," Rodney Wead said in '68. "But not today. The people no longer feel powerless and they fight back the way they can."

The next night, 26 businesses were damaged or looted, plus 37 vehicles. Ten people were injured, including four policemen.

Rioters targeted white-owned stores like Belzer's Market and Ruback's Market. Their Jewish owners had collectively been on North 24th Street for 51 years. But now they were done.

"You don't make a fortune and it's not worth losing your life," Marvin Belzer said.

Two days later, about the same time that actor Paul Newman stood atop a station wagon at Eppley Airfield and stumped for McCarthy, Beasley addressed a rally in the Safeway parking lot at 24th and Lake. He scolded the "thugs" who burned down his neighborhood.

Tensions flared again on North 24th Street on April 27, 1968.

He also spoke out against police brutality, which earned him a few quotes in news reports. Beasley started receiving angry calls and hate mail, even death threats.

Martin Luther King got it, you'll get it, too.

Don't worry about them, Chambers told Beasley. They're cowards. But Beasley had a young family. He packed up, left his hometown and spent the next five years in Philadelphia.

Chaos in North Omaha didn't distract Gibson. On May 1, he pitched 12 innings, beating the Astros 3-1.

John Beasley, left, and Dale Anders reported that police used excessive force in breaking up a dice game.

***

The day before the Nebraska primary, a downpour doused Omaha. Robert Kennedy rode up North 24th Street in a convertible, the rain soaking his head.

At Erskine, 1,500 people gathered in the street to hear the emerging voice of civil rights, the man who grieved with Coretta Scott King. The car stopped and Kennedy climbed a platform.

"Work with me so the next generation of black people has a better opportunity than you have had."

No state gave RFK a larger share of votes than Nebraska. He beat McCarthy, 52 percent to 31 percent — Vice President Hubert H. Humphrey wasn't on the ballot. Kennedy showed promise — Gale Sayers, Bill Russell and Hank Aaron endorsed him — but no single politician spoke for all blacks.

Two weeks later, Jackie Robinson, a disillusioned Republican desperate for inspiration, attended an interfaith banquet at the former bastion of segregation, Peony Park.

Diabetes weakened Robinson at 49 years old. But the man who inspired Bob Gibson to pick up a baseball still had pluck. Freedom, he said, is never given voluntarily by the oppressors. The oppressed must demand it.

Jackie Robinson, who cracked baseball's color barrier, spoke in Omaha May 28, 1968. Also pictured are Gary Gilmore, left, Tech athlete Ernie Britt, with medal, and Candy Wead.

"You will understand why we find it difficult to wait … when you have seen hate-filled policemen curse, kick, brutalize and even kill your black brothers and sisters with no punity. …

"When your first name becomes N----- and your middle name becomes 'boy' however old you are and your last name becomes 'John' and when your wife and mother are never given the respected title 'Mrs.' and when you are harmed by day and haunted by night by the fact that you are a Negro … never quite knowing what to expect next, and plagued with inner fears and outer resentment.

"There comes a time when the cup of endurance runs over, and men are no longer willing to be plunged into an abyss of injustice where they experience the bleakness of corroding despair."

Jackie's voice still mattered, but he couldn't stop the bleeding.

The next night in North Omaha, a black police officer shot and killed a Tech High junior who had stolen a car and resisted arrest. His name: Percy Hare, the younger brother of Tech's former basketball standout.

Six nights later, Robert F. Kennedy won the California primary, grabbing control of the Democratic nomination. He delivered his victory speech at the Ambassador Hotel, then walked through the hotel kitchen, where a Palestinian gunman fired three bullets into him.

When the news reached North Omaha the morning of June 5, blacks mourned RFK like one of their own. One business sold $1 Kennedy posters inscribed "Honorary Soul Brother."

"We can only hope that the well thinking Americans will put forth more effort to remove the causes that turn men into monsters," concluded an Omaha Star editorial.

On June 8, NBA star Oscar Robertson attended RFK's funeral in New York. The next day — Sunday afternoon — the Big O was in North O for Bryant Center's summer opening ceremony. Robertson, Bob Boozer (his old Olympic teammate)

Gale Sayers (left), Bob Boozer and Oscar Robertson headlined the Bryant Center's season opening, June 9, 1968.

and Gale Sayers signed autographs for the crowd, but they couldn't lift the mood.

From Emmett Till to Medgar Evers, the Birmingham church girls to Malcolm X, Dr. King to the Kennedy brothers, the body count of black heroes overwhelmed even the optimists, fueling depression and anger.

No one deployed anger like Bob Gibson.

***

On the day of Kennedy's death, a sparse crowd of 15,218 showed up at the new Astrodome — the "Eighth Wonder of the World" — to watch the Astros host the defending World Series champions.

Baseball's eighth wonder, the Cardinals ace, shut out the home team in a swift two hours, allowing just three hits. Thus began a streak of 47⅔ scoreless innings.

Gibson's filthy slider deserved much of the credit, he later wrote, but "I can't completely dismiss the fact that nobody gave me any s--- whatsoever for about two months after Bobby Kennedy died."

June 11: 9 innings, 0 runs. Cards 6, Braves 0.

The chip on Gibson's shoulder had long defined him. At All-Star games, he avoided the clubhouse because his fellow superstars wanted to mingle. He snapped at younger players who idolized him. And, most famously, he plunked hitters who dared take a home-run cut, including former teammates like Bill White.

"You son of a bitch," Gibson hollered at White after blasting his elbow with a heater, "you went for that outside ball! That part of the plate belongs to me!"

June 15: 9 innings, 0 runs. Cards 2, Reds 0.

Gibson always had arm talent. With incredibly strong legs, he coiled into a big windup, whirled and leapt at the hitter like a prizefighter throwing a knockout punch. And genetics gave him an edge — his forefinger and pinky were equal lengths, as were his ring and middle finger — so he naturally threw a cutter.

But Gibson didn't master the art of *pitching* until 1966 when he found precision. When Cardinals outfielder Mike Shannon moved to third base in '67, he asked Gibson where he should line up. Off the bag? On the line? The pitcher scolded him. *"I don't give a damn"* ... except when there's a righty batter with a runner on first and less than two outs. That's when Gibson's sinker would induce a ground ball to third.

June 20: 9 innings, 0 runs. Cards 1, Cubs 0.

Gibson's formula was simple. Pound the outside corner. Away. Away. Away. And if the hitter extends his arms too far, well, that's a sign of disrespect, punishable by 95-mph fastball in the back.

Think of a hitter as a dog with an electronic collar, Gibson later wrote. Sometimes he needs a slight jolt to restore discipline. Gibson presented a simpler metaphor if you prefer.

"Hitters were the enemy and the inside pitch was my warhead."

June 26: 9 innings, 0 runs. Cards 3, Cubs 0.

Gibson had a softer side. Two daughters. A basset hound named Snoopy. He built model cars and played the ukulele. But to batters, he remained mysterious.

They saw his sweaty brow — he wore a sweatshirt under his uniform, even in 100-degree heat.

They felt his squinty eyes — he needed glasses off the field.

Gibson didn't take social stands like Muhammad Ali, Jim Brown or Bill Russell. Constantly wary of people taking advantage of him, he resisted promoting his own community. In his mind, he represented nobody. He owed nobody.

But as the most dominant athlete at the whitest position in America's whitest sport, he couldn't avoid politics. Like it or not, he embodied the anger that white people saw in the streets. Which is why reporters — in the midst of civil unrest — didn't just want to ask him about baseball.

"The intention of riots," Gibson said, "is to get people to think and not to get complacent and take things for granted. Like a brushback pitch."

July 1: 9 innings, 1 run. Cards 5, Dodgers 1.

Hall of Famer and fellow Nebraskan Richie Ashburn knew that Gibson's stuff, especially his slider, put him in a class by himself. But it was Gibson's sneer — his "lack of concern for the welfare of the hitter" — that scared Ashburn when he stepped into the box.

"I always had the feeling I was standing there as the Grand Dragon of the Ku Klux Klan," Ashburn said.

Gibson recognized his image and his power. Unlike black men in the streets, he had an outlet for his anger.

Bob Gibson, owner of the supreme 1.12 ERA.

"I was a member of a race that had been intimidated by the white man for more than 200 years," Gibson wrote. "I had the opportunity, at last, to push off the mound in the other man's shoes."

July 6: 9 innings, 0 runs. Cards 3, Giants 0.

But his dominance came at a cost. Gibson's workload exerted so much stress on his elbow that he couldn't straighten his arm. Blood vessels ruptured. Muscles inflamed. Gibson needed medication to stay in the rotation.

"He has to have the highest threshold of pain I've ever seen in an athlete," the Cardinals trainer said. "But he never tells you how much he hurts." Gibson learned to use other arm muscles to compensate for those injured.

July 12: 9 innings, 1 run. Cards 8, Astros 1.

He did it all without help from home. The first time "Robert Gibson" appeared in newsprint was 1947 when an Omaha Star writer called him "Little Josh."

But by 1968, Bob had outgrown his father figure. Big brother couldn't resist telling him how to pitch and, as Bob wrote, "Josh didn't know a hell of a lot about pitching in the big leagues." The two bickered so often they stopped speaking.

"You've never seen anything until you've seen those two argue," nephew Fred Gibson said. "Oh my God. That's just how they love each other."

Josh's fire and stubbornness served him well as a coach, but they turned off those closest to him. Family still loved and respected him. They just couldn't get along with him.

"There were just moments in his life Uncle Josh had a falling-out with *everybody*," his nephew said.

July 21: 9 innings, 0 runs. Cards 2, Mets 0.

Of course, Josh's influence always extended beyond his family tree. He coached hundreds of kids in two decades. But in the late '60s, pushing 50 years old, Josh tossed his old glove in a closet and quit coaching, accelerating baseball's demise in North Omaha.

Tech High won a state championship in 1966 with kids who grew up learning from Josh. Without him a couple years later, the Trojans lost 33 straight games spanning three seasons.

"As soon as Josh Gibson was done, I was done," Tech coach John Morse said. "Because all the kids I got, they didn't even know how to put on a baseball uniform. They didn't have no midget uniforms. Nothing. ... I couldn't win a game."

July 25: 9 innings, 0 runs. Cards 5, Phillies 0.

As Bob Gibson rolled through summer, his neighborhood took another fastball to the gut.

***

Through droughts and floods, assassinations and riots, devastating wars and the Great Depression, the "Big Four" didn't stop.

Armour, Cudahy, Swift and Wilson had slaughtered more than half a billion animals since the 1880s, feeding the world and anchoring Omaha's economy.

By 1968, they couldn't keep up. New competitors built small, automated facilities in small towns and the Big Four struggled to modernize. Cudahy ceased slaughtering in '67. But the biggest blow came in the summer of '68 when the biggest meatpacking plant, Armour, closed.

Since 1897, Armour stood like a brick fortress, stretching four blocks along Q Street. Even at the end, it employed 2,500 — one-third of the packinghouse workforce. Armour's impact on the local economy reached $200 million a year — $1.5 billion in today's dollars.

"Times change," Mayor A.V. Sorensen said. "There is no status quo in industry."

Just two years earlier, Sorensen and stockyards executives had expressed optimism. Now another 750 blacks needed jobs.

By the late '60s, packinghouses like Armour were so decayed that "you could take your pen and slide it in between the bricks and the mortar would fall out," one worker said. Armour was razed in 1971.

Vice President Humphrey, left, and Omaha Mayor A.V. Sorensen in 1968.

"Oh my god, it was like a bomb going off," said Cathy Hughes, whose husband worked the kill floor at Cudahy. "The workers were not prepared."

As the industry collapsed, unemployment rates in North Omaha jumped as high as 25 percent, according to one report. And those who found jobs didn't make the same money.

The irony? As packing plants emptied, city planners were literally paving the way to the stockyards. In 1954, just before Omaha became No. 1 in the world, Mayor Johnny Rosenblatt wanted to accelerate the cattle commute from north of the city.

He proposed a new expressway connecting the Mormon Bridge to Q Street. The path eventually shifted through neighborhoods on the Near North Side, where land was cheaper.

North Freeway construction in 1968 disrupted the neighborhood.

Beginning in 1966, bulldozers demolished hundreds of dilapidated homes north of Cuming Street, despite protests. Homeowners received market value, but it wasn't much. Without an open housing law, overcrowding in North Omaha intensified.

Apartments aren't good enough, one woman said during a protest meeting. "We are used to a home, a yard and green grass."

The freeway's biggest problem was its location: between 27th and 28th Streets. The concrete path rolled out of downtown and ripped through the black community.

Remember Pinkney Street, the old home of Gibson, Ed Danner, Johnny Rodgers, Rodney Wead, Dick Davis, Gale Sayers? The freeway cut it in half.

"It was a huge deal," John Beasley said. "I think it was by design. They killed 30th Street and they killed 24th Street. You didn't have to drive down those streets anymore."

By '68, it was pretty clear the stockyards no longer needed an artery to Interstate 680. But freeway construction crawled through the '70s and '80s until residents of Miller Park, Minne Lusa and Florence — white neighborhoods in the path of the bulldozers — resisted and won. That's why the North Freeway stopped just north of the black neighborhood, at a street coincidentally named for the 1968 mayor, Sorensen Parkway.

The freeway, Roger Sayers said, did nothing but damage neighborhood character, commerce and unity.

"A road to nowhere."

Police brutality. Assassinations. Commercial decay. Exploding unemployment. It all set the stage for aggressive leadership.

In July 1968, the voice of Black Power walked into Omaha's favorite ballpark. Stokely Carmichael came to see his wife, a South African singer, participate in the "Salute to Jazz" at Rosenblatt Stadium. During an Omaha Star interview, Carmichael argued against integration — "subterfuge for the maintenance of white supremacy."

"If blacks accept that a decent house or education depends on moving into a white neighborhood or sending their children to a white school, they reinforce the idea that blacks are inferior." To retain their culture, he said, blacks must shed their colonial status and create a separate society.

Carmichael's views didn't represent most blacks. Whitney Young, national Urban League director, argued that self-imposed segregation only echoed white bigots. But Black Power quickly gained momentum.

In Omaha, Carmichael met with Ernie Chambers, whom he admired. He also met with the Black Panthers, who'd opened a chapter in North Omaha in 1968. The California-based group initiated social and educational programs. They also saw themselves as neighborhood defenders, strapping guns like soldiers in Vietnam.

"Now that the Black Panthers are in Omaha," a July press release stated in the Star, "the white police force will no longer be able to ride roughshod over the Blacks in this community without paying a heavy price."

J. Edgar Hoover took notice. The FBI director, who'd called the Panthers "the greatest threat to the internal security of the country," ordered surveillance on the North Omaha Panthers.

Ernie Chambers

Ernie Chambers loves a good metaphor. But even by his standards, he got creative in September 1968.

A group of local students — mostly white — interviewed him for YOUTH magazine and Chambers described blacks' distrust for whites.

"Suppose you're a baby rabbit. Foxes chase rabbits and eat them. Well maybe a baby rabbit and a baby fox will play together until the rabbit's mother teaches him this important lesson: it was one of those foxes who deprived you of a father.

"Now the fox feels mistreated and says, 'I'm playing with him. I'm not like the rest of the foxes.' But as he grows older and lives around foxes, certain instincts are naturally going to assert themselves. And he's going to be pressured by the older foxes.

"He's going to see them eating rabbits; none of them are playing with rabbits; rabbits always run from them. And since he can't live with the foxes and run with the rabbits, he has to live with the foxes and eat the rabbits.

"So this little rabbit is in a better position if he is taught to beware of all foxes. All foxes."

Across the nation, law enforcement had a busy summer. Three white cops and four black men died in a Cleveland shootout. New York policemen attacked black militants at a Brooklyn courthouse as, not coincidentally, blacks were on trial for attacking policemen.

In August, about 700 people gathered at Omaha's Fontenelle Park for the "founding convention of the Nebraska Peace and Freedom Party," a black organization. Chambers received the loudest applause.

"To me, black power is a well-loaded gun in the hands of an angry black man who recognizes who the real enemy is."

Amid the violence, a new motto swept the nation. A political slogan advocating a crackdown on urban militance: "Law and order." Time Magazine declared it the No. 1 campaign issue of the presidential election, bigger than Vietnam.

To whites, conservatives especially, the phrase was a rallying cry to restore safety to cities.

"We talk of sending a man to the moon," candidate Ronald Reagan said in one of his loudest applause lines, "but we can't even send a man safely across the park."

Demonstrators confront a row of National Guard soldiers during the Democratic National Convention in Chicago, Aug. 26, 1968.

To blacks, the phrase was a dog whistle.

"Law and order is just the new way to yell n-----," black comedian Dick Gregory said.

Of course, law and order wasn't just a racial issue. It was cultural. Protests turned violent on campuses from Cal-Berkeley to Columbia University.

The touchstone came during the Democratic National Convention in Chicago, where police clashed with demonstrators, filling the streets with mayhem. It was like the Wallace night at Civic Auditorium — times 100. For four nights, bloodshed captivated a national TV audience, overshadowing Humphrey's nomination.

"Americans now know — because they have seen it with their own eyes — that what black people have been saying about police abuses is true," Whitney Young wrote in a column printed in the Omaha Star. "For a change, black skulls weren't being cracked. Those were white middle-class youngsters who felt the sting of the gas and the crack of the bully club."

Late '60s students at Franklin School line up to get their swings in a ball game.

***

One week after the mayhem in Chicago, school started in Omaha.

The Omaha Star pressured school administrators on the contents of Central High history textbooks and North High cheerleading eligibility standards, which effectively banned blacks. A subtler form of conflict festered at the neighborhood borders.

Franklin School on 35th Street was the first teaching job for Sam Crawford, a graduate of Tuskegee College in Alabama. He came north in the summer of 1966 because Omaha Public Schools needed black teachers for black students.

That fall, Franklin was 41 percent black. Two years later, it was 65 percent black. But shifting demographics didn't ruin Franklin's educational culture; growing distrust did. Everyone feared everyone.

Black kids feared going to school because they might be beaten or shot by police. White teachers feared going to work because blacks might riot or bomb the school. Crawford's principal, who took over Franklin when it was nearly all-white, often called him to her office just to sit.

"I guess she felt like I protected her."

Many black students exploited the fear, Crawford said. They could get away with disobedience because administrators and teachers didn't want to deal with them — or their parents. They stopped listening to adults entirely. At night, students saw the riots on their TVs and felt emboldened.

"Empowered," Crawford said. "That's the word."

So what did white families do in that environment? They fled. Moved to the suburbs — and built new suburbs beyond. What did white teachers do? They quit. They wanted to teach geometry and English, not play social worker and security guard.

"A lot of the best teachers left their schools," Crawford said. "They didn't want to deal with it."

The most damaging loss wasn't a white teacher, but a black one.

Bob Rose, who grew up without a father in the South Omaha projects, spent 15 years guiding athletes at Howard Kennedy Grade School and Horace Mann Junior High. Kids like Jerry Bartee, the future Cardinals minor leaguer.

Bartee grew up without a father, too, but he received more than his share of discipline. Rose wore a whistle with a rawhide strap and when a kid screwed up, he ordered him to touch his knees. *Whack.*

At the end of eighth grade, Bartee finally got the nerve to ask Mr. Rose, "Why me?"

"He looked me dead in the eyes and he said, 'Bartee, as long as I'm talking *to* you, I care *about* you. When I stop talking to you, you need to be concerned.'

"From that moment on, I wanted Mr. Rose to ride me like a horse because I wanted him to always care about me."

Over the next year, Mr. Rose escorted Bartee's class to lunch and every day he ordered a fruit cocktail cup. "Every day!" Bartee said. "He'd take that spoon and he'd take a bite of fruit cocktail and then he'd tap twice on his cup. I started to eat fruit cocktail that way."

The last day of ninth grade, Mr. Rose asked Bartee what he was going to do after high school. Jerry hemmed and hawed. At 14, he didn't have the nerve to give a straight answer.

"How do you tell somebody you want to be like him? But I did. I ended up being a gym teacher."

And then he became Creighton's head baseball coach. And then Omaha South principal. And then OPS assistant superintendent.

Rose didn't have those opportunities. In the summer of '68 — a few months after the Wallace riots and the walkout at Mann — Rose's old college friend called with a proposal. He worked for State Farm in Denver and wanted Rose to join him. Help integrate Denver's insurance market.

"He had a chance to make more money," Rose's son said.

Rose deserved a grand farewell. He barely said goodbye. When school started in September, he was gone. Off to an integrated neighborhood in Colorado with his wife, kids and — for a few weeks — a 22-year-old houseguest, the same cousin he introduced to sports in the mid-'50s.

Marlin Briscoe slept in Rose's basement.

***

On Sept. 2, Gibson won his 20th game, blanking the Reds in 10 innings. His ERA dropped to 0.99. St. Louis, en route to 97 wins, had a 13-game lead in the National League and two hands on the pennant.

But baseball didn't best showcase North Omaha's athletic talent in 1968. Neither did basketball, despite the exploits of Bob Boozer and Ron Boone. Which sport was king? Football.

In Lincoln, Bob Devaney's top two rushers, Joe Orduna and Dick Davis, came from the neighborhood.

Gale Sayers was the NFL's best running back. His younger brother, Ron Sayers, led UNO in rushing in '67 and '68 — the Chargers drafted Ronnie 44th overall in '69.

At Tech High, a 5-foot-10, 170-pound senior tailback broke six Metro Conference records, including 20 touchdowns in one season. Before Nebraskans called him "The Jet," Johnny Rodgers' teammates called him "Mr. S" — that's short for Superman.

Omaha Tech standout Johnny Rodgers.

From left, Johnny Ray, Johnny Rodgers, Paul Griego and Robert Faulkner at Tech High in 1967.

Red-hot Summer

But only one Omahan made football history in 1968.

To call Briscoe an underdog would be an understatement. Yes, pro scouts knew about him coming out of UNO. One New Orleans Saints evaluator said Briscoe had "the greatest arm I have ever seen on any quarterback — college or pro."

"He's the only man I have ever seen who can run to his left and throw the ball right-handed 55 yards through the air with complete accuracy."

Rookie starting quarterback Marlin Briscoe warming up for a game in 1968.

But Briscoe was 5-foot-10 and black, two major disqualifications. The Broncos drafted him in the 14th round with no intention of letting him throw passes. In their eyes, he was a cornerback.

"The chances of Marlin Briscoe becoming the first Negro quarterback in NFL-AFL football appear infinitesimally small," World-Herald columnist Wally Provost wrote.

Briscoe admitted being nervous over the prospect of becoming a pioneer. "It's scared me. I'll have to show them that I have mental leadership first. A quarterback's brainpower is respected first. Mechanics second."

At training camp in July, coaches gave him a token quarterback tryout. But after Briscoe pulled his hamstring running sprints, Denver sent him back to defense.

Then began an improbable run of quarterback misfortune. Broncos starter Steve Tensi broke his collarbone in the preseason. Then three backups tried and failed. Denver staggered to an 0-2 start.

On Tuesday, Sept. 24, the desperate Denver coach, Lou Saban, approached Briscoe on the practice field and broke the news. *You're moving to quarterback.*

Saban wasn't quite ready to pull the trigger, though. Not until the Broncos fell behind the Patriots 17-10 and his starter threw an interception early in the fourth quarter. With 9:53 left, No. 15 in orange trotted onto the field. His first play, Briscoe completed a 22-yard pass. The Broncos stalled and missed a field goal.

The next drive, Marlin the Magician engineered a 5-play, 80-yard drive, scrambling for a 12-yard TD.

"I'm out there playing sandlot ball," Briscoe recalled. "My mindset was: Play just like I did at OU."

The Broncos ran out of time and lost 20-17 and not everyone loved the experiment — "Running like he did against us will make him a poor insurance risk," one Boston player said.

But back in Omaha, Briscoe's fourth quarter sent shockwaves down North 24th Street. The moment still doesn't feel real.

White people didn't understand, said Dorothea Moore, Marlin's cousin. Still don't. The looks that blacks received walking into stores. The obstacles they confronted going to schools or voting booths. The perceptions that blacks weren't smart enough to lead or to handle pressure.

On rare occasions when Moore saw a black person on TV who wasn't portrayed as a clown or a criminal, she called her friends with excitement.

Now, the last week of September 1968, imagine ... Bob Gibson was baseball's best pitcher and Marlin Briscoe was the first black quarterback. Two North Omahans appearing on her TV *at the two most racially restrictive positions in sports.*

Moore still weeps remembering what her cousin Marlin meant to the black teachers and preachers, the nurses and maids, the mechanics and pack-inghouse workers. All the hard-working men and women who "wanted something out of life." It wasn't just hope, Moore said, it was dignity.

"It's a light that glistens from within that tells you, 'I am not dirt. I am a human being. And I have respect.' "

Briscoe debuted Sept. 29, the same afternoon that Sayers rushed for 108 yards and one touchdown against Minnesota. Two days later, the newspaper of record — the New York Times — featured gobs of World Series hype. Buried beneath horse racing results, readers found a one-paragraph dispatch from the Associated Press:

Briscoe created a little magic in his first game as a pro quarterback.

> *Coach Lou Saban of the Denver Broncos said today that Marlin Briscoe, the first Negro ever to play quarterback in the American Football League, would start Sunday against the Cincinnati Bengals.*

On Oct. 2, Gibson struck out 17 Tigers in Game 1 of the World Series.

Two days later, Johnny Rodgers scored touchdowns of 85, 65 and 24 yards for Tech High against Council Bluffs Thomas Jefferson. The next night, Bob Boozer led the Chicago Bulls to an exhibition win over Milwaukee with 30 points.

It was all building to Oct. 6.

Chapter 10

Dark Side of the Moon

BEFORE THE SUN ROSE on a crisp fall day in North Omaha, the full moon disappeared.

At 6:10 a.m. in the western sky, a white ball slipped into Earth's 900,000-mile shadow, darker and darker until it vanished, reappearing blood red. For 63 minutes, half the world witnessed a full lunar eclipse.

Marines saw it in Vietnam after sweeping the jungles near Da Nang, unaware that LBJ was about to jump-start Paris peace talks by halting bombs over Hanoi.

Olympians saw it as they boarded planes for Mexico City, including sprinters still considering a boycott. "We have no intention of disrupting the Games," sprinter John Carlos said. "But that does not mean we will not do something to accentuate the injustices that have been done to the black man in America."

Astronauts saw it in Cape Kennedy, Florida, as they prepared for Apollo 8's Christmas trip orbiting the same moon.

Gale Sayers, the NFL's marquee player, might have spotted the phenomenon over breakfast in Baltimore, where he prepared to face the league's marquee team, the Baltimore Colts.

Sixteen hundred miles west, Marlin Briscoe had a better view of the eclipse — if he was willing to wake up early. Briscoe began that Sunday morning with a blank slate, hours from his first professional start at quarterback.

Who didn't see the eclipse on Sunday, Oct. 6, 1968? Bob Gibson. The Detroit skies were too gray, the pitcher too weary from the worst night he'd ever spent in a hotel.

Eleven hours before he took the mound for Game 4 of the World Series — St. Louis led the series 2-1 — Gibson woke up to strangers pounding on his hotel room door. "Telegram!" Tiger fans had found him. The noise continued for 30 minutes. Then Gibson got a prank phone call, "Is Denny McLain there?"

That's a name Gibson heard over and over in '68.

The affable, white Detroit ace won an astounding 31 games in "the year of the pitcher." He was the kind of guy who delivered an impromptu piano concert in a hotel lobby the night before his World Series debut. The kind of guy who delivered a meatball to Mickey Mantle in the slugger's final career at-bat in Detroit — Mantle hammered it over the right-field wall.

"I would have dropped my pants on the mound before I would have deferred to an opposing player that way," Gibson later wrote. "My method of showing respect for a guy like Mantle would have been to reach back for something extra with which to blow his ass away, if I could."

"But I guess that's why McLain was on the cover of Time and I was still borrowing money from insurance policies."

1968:
A year of North stars

It's touchdown time for Sayers ... who steps seven yards in the first qua...
—AP Wire...

...oozer Hits 33 Points Before Record Turnout

NBA Standings

Eastern Division				Western Division			
	W	L	G.B.		W	L	G.B.
...phia	49	17		St. Louis	46	29	4½
...sm	44	20	4	S. Frisco	39	28	
...ton	34	31	13½	L. An's	37	27	
...icago	31	35	16½	Chicago	19	46	25½
...innati	31	35	18½	Seattle	18	47	
...troit	25	37	20½	S. Diego	15	52	30½

Results Tuesday

Cincinnati	116		Louis	115
...timore	127	(o't.)	Detroit	124
...go	124		Boston	117
...w York	115	(o'vt.)	San Fran.	112

American Association

...tsburgh	119		Denver	104
...innesota	119		Anaheim	117
...allas	148		Oakland	130

Games Tonight

Seattle-Chicago at Baltimore
San Francisco at Baltimore
...Boston at Los Angeles

New York (AP) — Bob
Boozer climaxed a stirring
Chicago rally at the end of
regulation play and again in
overtime Tuesday night as
the Bulls staggered Detroit,
124-121 before a record National Basket Ball Association
crowd.

Dick Barnett shot New York
ahead to stay at the start of
an overtime period and kept
...there for a 115-112

Chicago trailed ...fore Boozer, Jerr... Clem Haskins... straight points to ...to 109-108 with a... in the fourth peri...

Boozer sent th... an extra period v... six seconds befor...

With a sellout... 19,500 looking o... er scored sev... points in the ove... ing the Bulls' la...

Chicago

	F	G	T
Boozer	4	7-9	15
M'Lem	4	1-2	9
Washton	6	3-4	13
Ericson	7	2-4	16
Sloan	4	4-5	12
Robnson	4	6-7	20
Haskins	9	0-0	9
Barnes	1	2-3	
Clemsns		1-2	3
Totals	**49**	**26-36**	**124**

Chicago ... ...ning. C...
Detroit ... Fouled out—Chicago...
Total fouls—Chicago...
Attendance—19,500.

Gibson's Fast Ball Is Hailed

Philadelphia, Pa. (AP) — Bob
Gibson said he may have
thrown harder when he was
younger, but never straighter
than he did Monday night.

Gibson beat the Philadelphia
Phillies for his fifteenth consecutive victory and tenth shutout.

The 32-year-old right-hander
of the St. Louis Cardinals
blanked the Phillies, 2-0. He
posted his eighteenth triumph
against five defeats.

His shut-out tied a club record
set in 1942 by Mort Cooper and
left him six shy of the major

Gibson book to be published October 8, Page 22.

...for whitewashes — 16 by Grover ...exander of the 1916

...so is only two vic... ...from the 17 straight ...by ElRoy Face of ...gh Pirates, who did ...ief pitcher. The all... ...d is 19 straight by J... ...of the New York ...1888 and R... ...he 1912 Gian... ...ter Than Ko... ...g question i... ...ubhouse afte... ...ther Gibson ...night thar ...game th... ...her never was ...had great co... ...Ien in the...

Sayers Ties Bear Recor...

Chicago Daily News Service.

Bloomington, Minn. — As Jim
Dooley said, after his Chicago
Bears had won:

"This game was a matter of
existence - - of survival - - for
us. If we had lost, we'd have
been three games behind. We
had to win to stay in the race."

But there was a moment, with
...:21 left in Sunday's 27-17 vic...ory over Minnesota, when he
...anced around at his battered
...fensive team and found them
...oking "shocked and
...wildered."

The Vikings had narrowed a
...3 Bear lead to 20-17, and all
...momentum was going
...inst the Bears. "It looked..." ...Brian Piccolo said later,
...re we were falling apart."
...ere was good reason. Bear
...terbacks Jack Concannon a...
...Rudy Bukich had been
...out by shoulder injuries
...were merely spectators,
...ng on the sidelines.

"Be Careful"

No. 1 Fullback Ronnie Bull
hadn't played all day because of
a leg injury. His only helpful
activity had been to assist Dr.
Ted Fox, the team physician, in
setting Concannon's broken
collarbone in the dressing room.

Dooley rallied his men before
they took the field, after Minnesota had narrowed the lead to
three points.

"We're not losing," he
reminded them. "We're still
ahead. I want you to take that
ball the length of the field."

He told his only remaining
quarterback—Larry Rakestraw:

"Be careful. Go with the running game, because we have no
more quarterbacks. Control the
ball."

It seemed almost impossible,
but they did it, not only holding
the ball for 6:51. but scoring a
touchdown that sealed Minnesota's first loss...

108 for Gale

Even Gale Sayers, No. 1 B
weapon, was shaken up half
through the march, and had
turn over his job to Piccolo,
an all-substitute backfield.

Sayers rushed for 108 ya...
and a touchdown in 16 carrie...
It was game No. 13 of 100-p...
yardage, matching a tea...
record held by Rick Casares.

Chicago	14	6 0 7—27
Minnesota	0	3 7 7—
Chi—Sayers 7 run (Percival kick).		
Chi—Gordon 15 pass from Concann...		
(Percival kick).		
Chi—FG Percival 43.		
Minn—FG Cox 45.		
Minn-Washington 22 pass from C'zar...		
(Cox kick).		
Chi—Kurek 23 run (Cox kick).		
Minn-Percival 11 run (Percival kick).		
Attendance—47,693.		

Statistics	Bears	Vikings
First downs	19	
Rushing yardage	273	12
Passing yardage	131	121
Return yardage		
Passes		
Intercepted by	14-20	12-25
Punts		
Fumbles lost	3-38	4-3
Yards penalized	124	3-7

Rodgers's 3 Scores Lead Tech Parade

...Burke Yields To 3d-Rated Rival by 35-0

Results Wednesday

...ch	35	Burke	0
...vder	33	Fort Calhoun	0
...lleview	32	Weeping Water	6
...usville	19	Bennington	0
...horn	19	Blair	13
		Valley	12

By Tom Ash

...took Tech High a while to
...t up on a chilly Wednesday
...t, but the Trojans burned
...ke in the second half for a
football victory at Burke
...dium.

...e third-ranked Trojans (6-1)
...n 342 yards, all on the
...nd, while holding Burke
...to 78 yards passing and
...s one rushing.

...was the same familiar story
...he Trojan attack—Johnny
...ers. The flying halfback
...ed for 181 yards on 21 car...and recorded his fourth
...touchdown game of the

...ers has 98 points—with
...mes left. If he keeps up
...ce, he will break the
...litan Conference season
...record of 121 set by Boys
...Nate McKinney last...

...'s got the Trojans off
...g start with a 26-yard
...first time he carried
...But John Ray's lost
...to the end zone o...

The Trojan defense was near...ly as tough the second half, buy...ing the attack until plenty of
time. Burke did not cross mid...field until the fourth quarter
then only with the aid of a
roughing penalty on punter Bob...by Nocita.

Two pass interceptions by
Tech's David Bennings in the
final period chilled the only
Burke threats.

Tech stoked up with three
touchdowns in the fourth
after Quarterback Paul ...
sneaked over in the thir...
a 76-yard march.

The Trojans showed
awesome speed at the sta...
the final quarter. On st...
down with 19 to go for the
down at their own 29, Rod...
broke for 24 yards. Ja...
Greene picked up 8 and Rodg...
13.

After a holding penalty, R...
gers gained 10 and Greene ...
Larry Tavis picked up the fir...
down and Rodgers sailed aroun...
his left end for a 10-yard touch...
down.

Rodgers cruised the other side
moments later for a 27-yard
score after Nocita was smeared
on a punt atte...

Omaha Stars Sparkle

A couple of Omahans shared the sports spotlight Monday night
Bob Gibson continued his torrid pitching streak to pace the St.
Louis Cardinals and Gale Sayers added a scoring streak of his own
to pace the Chicago Bears to a National Football League win.
Gibson won his fifteenth consecutive game, a two-hitter over Philadelphia, 2-0. Sayers bolted 76 yards on Chicago's second play from
scrimmage to score the Bear... ...own in a 10-7 win over

Ron Boone Propels Dallas to ABA Win

By the Associated Press.

Ron Boone scored 11 of his
27 points in the last 5½ minutes
Thursday night to lift Dallas
past New York, 110-103. in an
American Basket Ball Association game at Commack, N. Y.

Boone. former Omaha Tech
High ace. scored three basket...
after New York had crept with...
in 101-99 with 1:50 left.

...Minnesota. behind Connie Ha...
...umped Miam...

Briscoe Gets His Chance And Makes the Most of It

Former Omaha University
quarterback Marlin Briscoe became the first Negro ever to
play quarterback in the American Football League Sunday
and left the fans hollering for
more.

Inserted in the lineup in the
fourth quarter of the Denver
Broncos 20-17 loss to Boston,
Briscoe scored a touchdown on
a 12-yard run after running 19
yards to set it up. He received...

Briscoe Is Handed A Very Big Order

...DS of football fans in the realm of the Central Inter-
...Conference will be interested in how Omahan Marlin
...s today in his first quarterback start for the Denver
...the opposition. Paul Brown's Cincinnati Benga...
...horough test

Gibson hadn't lost his edge, despite reaching a level that astonished even his opponents. Following Game 1, Tigers manager Mayo Smith said that asking him about Gibson's 17 strikeouts was "like asking Mrs. Lincoln how she liked the play."

"The fans never doubt the outcome of a Gibson-pitched game," a Detroit columnist wrote. "Their confidence is so complete they take the seventh-inning stretch in the fifth."

Back home, the 12-page weekly Omaha Star devoted two full pages commemorating the record performance — "All Omaha is proud of Bob Gibson." What could he possibly do next?

The greatest afternoon in North Omaha sports history awaited and it broke down like this: Cardinals-Tigers at noon on channel 3, followed by Broncos-Bengals at 3 p.m. Between them on channel 6, Bears faced the Colts at 1 p.m.

Not the best day for 11 a.m. church services, huh?

Imagine the poor souls at Zion Baptist squiggling in the pews during Rev. McNair's sermon. Or the folks at Hope Lutheran checking their watches as the organist, Mrs. Bailey, starts the fourth verse of "Amazing Grace."

Hallelujah! Now let's find a TV!

***

Tiger Stadium looked like the beginning scenes of Genesis 7.

There was no sign of Noah, but two famous men soaked in the front row: Hubert H. Humphrey and Jackie Robinson.

The vice president had met Gibson during a White House dinner in '67. Following Game 1, he phoned the MVP in the Cardinals clubhouse.

"I'm with you all the way," Humphrey said.

He wasn't lying. The Democratic nominee flew from Washington, D.C., to watch Game 4 from the commissioner's box. He brought Robinson, who'd changed his party affiliation since the spring.

"The election of Nixon," Robinson told reporters on the plane, "would be death to the blacks."

Omaha World-Herald

Sports Section

OMAHA, NEB., MONDAY, OCTOBER 7, 1968

Gibson, Humphrey . . . 'hope to get together.'   —UPI Telephoto.

Gibson with one of his biggest fans, Democratic presidential nominee Hubert H. Humphrey.

Nixon, who owned a big lead in the polls, issued a national radio address that morning rebuking Humphrey's "Marshall Plan for the cities," a bold promise to "ensure that no American will have to live in poverty." Nixon didn't buy it.

New government programs to help the poor, he said, would "drain the Federal Treasury to soothe the public conscience." The greatest reservoir of neglected resources, Nixon said, is "the energies and spirit of the American people themselves."

Political debates could wait.

After a 37-minute rain delay and Marvin Gaye's elegant national anthem, St. Louis started fast. Lou Brock smashed McLain's second pitch over the wall. Home run.

Gibson rolled through the first two innings, but in the top of the third, the gloomy sky opened again on 53,000 Tiger fans still seeking a crack in Gibson's armor. Their best hope was the rain.

Umpires called for the tarp, and Gibson retreated to his sanctuary in the Cardinals clubhouse. He kicked off his muddy spikes, shed his wet No. 45 jersey and changed his undershirt. He turned an ear to the radio and his mouth to a vanilla swirl.

A starting pitcher hates to warm up, throw two innings and then — just as his team grabs a 4-0 lead — stiffen up. Especially Gibson, whose aching left leg and burning right elbow had racked up 324 innings in six months. Gibson relieved his pain with sugar.

One ice cream cone. Then another. Then another.

Back in North Omaha, the sun shined through living room windows. Savvy sports fans bypassed the rain delay and turned to channel 6, where Sayers confronted the mighty Baltimore defense.

At 25, Sayers had earned first-team all-pro his first three NFL seasons. Teams so desired him that owner/coach George Halas spent the offseason shaking his head at trade offers, including one rumored deal with the New York Giants.

Nine players for Sayers? Halas circulated a press release, tongue in cheek.

"For the sixth time since early in January, the Bears today categorically denied that Gale Sayers has been traded to the New York Giants. ... Sayers is a positive untouchable and is not for sale or trade. The only market on which he can be found is the stock market with Paine, Webber, Jackson and Curtis on LaSalle Street."

Sayers spent the offseason working as Paine Webber's first black broker, but the Bears were a bad bet against Don Shula's juggernaut Colts.

A scoreless first quarter offered a glimmer of hope. Then, early in the second, Chicago faced second-and-2 at its 41. That's when Sayers reminded fans why they didn't run to the bathroom when he ran on the field.

No. 40 in white took a handoff and swept right, his right hand gripping the ball like a quarterback. When he reached a wall of blue defenders, Sayers planted his right foot four yards in the backfield and cut back inside, switching the ball to his left hand.

Two steps — left, right — then he saw a chute. Sayers planted his left foot and cut back, splitting the Colts defense and turning on the burners, all the way to the end zone.

Years later, Sayers called it the greatest run of his career. Poor Bubba Smith, Baltimore Colts all-pro defensive end, missed him twice.

"It was like one of those old silent movie chase scenes ..." Sayers wrote. "The farmer trying to cross the road gets knocked on his rear by the bandits' car whizzing by. Then he starts crossing the road again and gets knocked over by a police car. ... Bubba and I could've had a conversation. ...

"I have to say it myself, I made a helluva run."

The Colts won 28-7, but Sayers finished with 105 yards, expanded his league lead in rushing yards and created a highlight for his eventual Hall of Fame induction.

That day was coming sooner than anyone expected.

***

"Is Denny McLain there?"

Not anymore. During the 75-minute rain delay at the World Series, the Tigers' 31-game winner asked not to pitch again. He couldn't raise his arm above his head.

Gibson couldn't fathom sitting out. He finished his third or fourth vanilla cone, emerged from the clubhouse and walked to his bullpen. He lobbed two pitches like an old man before firing five fastballs that, according to his bullpen catcher, "burned the hell out of my hand." Play resumed and Gibson wiped the Tigers in the third.

Then he belted a home run to lead off the fourth. 5-0.

That's when the game turned goofy. St. Louis, worried about another downpour, rushed toward the fifth inning to make the score official, deliberately giving away outs on the bases. Detroit, hoping for postponement, stalled as long as possible.

Detroit fans chanted: "Rain, rain, rain."

As the temperature dropped into the 40s, fans could see Gibson's breath as he stomped the ground, trying to dislodge mud from his cleats. He gave up a fourth-inning homer, then retired nine straight batters.

"You have to hand it to Gibson," comedian Bob Hope joked later, "it's not easy to strike out 10 men while treading water."

By the seventh inning, the Cardinals led 6-1 and Jackie Robinson had seen enough. He stood up and looked at the vice president. "I'm leaving."

Too bad Jackie couldn't have gone immediately to Denver. At almost that exact time, Marlin Briscoe trotted onto the field at Mile High Stadium.

Briscoe thought of Robinson often as his first start approached. If he failed, Briscoe knew it would only fortify racial barriers. Reinforce stereotypes. And black quarterbacks behind him would have it even tougher.

"It would be unfair to think he is going to become the Moses to lead the Broncos out of the wilderness," one Denver columnist wrote before the game.

Marlin Briscoe (15) switched from cornerback to quarterback following a string of bad Bronco luck.

"Briscoe is too inexperienced to be tossed to the wolves this early," said another.

Skeptics got it right. Briscoe, hampered by a thin playbook, struggled through the first half. He completed 4 of 11 passes and the offense didn't cross the 50-yard line.

At halftime, coach Lou Saban benched him in favor of regular starter Steve Tensi, still recovering from a broken collarbone. Denver rallied to a 10-7 win but the sports world barely noticed.

Back in Detroit, Gibson commanded all the attention. He cleaned up the slop at Tiger Stadium, a 10-1 Cardinals win. His seventh consecutive World Series victory — all complete games — broke another record. Afterward, Humphrey visited the clubhouse and Gibson gave him a copy of his new autobiography, "Ghetto to Glory."

The Cardinals held a 3-1 series lead and most figured Gibson — on the verge of becoming the three-time World Series MVP — had thrown his last pitch of 1968. His right elbow throbbed.

"I sure hope it ends tomorrow."

"We are caught in a vicious cycle and time is running out. Our people need decent housing — now. To afford such housing they need meaningful job opportunities — now. To obtain better jobs they must have better education — now. And so the circle continues. Failure to act courageously on these key needs together — and to act soon — will almost certainly lead to urban collapse and to a national crisis that we dare not contemplate."

— Omaha Star, October 1968

The sun rose again Monday morning — 7:27 a.m. Kids walked to school and parents drove to work and a brilliant white moon set without notice.

Change happens fast in a game. It's harder to define within a neighborhood. But by Oct. 7, 1968, a dark shadow consumed North Omaha.

Political leaders died. Critical mentors exited. Guns and firebombs stamped a stigma on 24th and Lake, once the glorious heartbeat of the neighborhood. Businesses abandoned the area. Bulldozers leveled homes and packinghouses. By the end of the October, Swift announced its last day of meatpacking, too — another 1,700 jobs vanished.

North Omaha wasn't the same after 1968. Neither was its epic generation of athletes.

The Tigers won Game 5 of the World Series, 5-3. They won Game 6 in St. Louis, too, setting up a winner-take-all finale.

Just as he did in '64 and '67, Gibson took the ball in Game 7. He dominated, striking out five Tigers through three innings. He retired 20 of the first 21 hitters. With two outs in the seventh — the game still scoreless — Norm Cash and Willie Horton lashed back-to-back singles.

Then one crack of the bat silenced Busch Stadium.

Jim Northrup, who homered off Gibson in Game 4, ripped the first pitch to center field. Curt Flood, the Cardinals' six-time Gold Glover, took a few steps in, but the white shirts behind home plate concealed the ball. When he finally spotted it, Flood changed direction, slipped on the wet grass and let the ball sail over his head for a two-run triple.

For years, Gibson and Flood had roomed together on the road, enduring racist hecklers, restaurants and hotels. When the inning ended, they passed on the way to the dugout. "It was my fault," Flood told him. "It was nobody's fault," Gibson replied.

The Cardinals lost Game 7, 4-1.

On Oct. 16, American sprinters Tommie Smith and John Carlos climbed the medal stand in Mexico City, bowed their heads and raised their black-gloved fists in protest — the enduring image of the '68 Olympics. The International Olympic Committee banned Smith and Carlos from the remainder of the Games.

Two days later, Gibson received another motorcade through North Omaha. This time it was bittersweet. Major League Baseball responded to "the year of the pitcher" with major rule modifications. It lowered the mound, shrunk the strike zone and restricted inside pitches.

A Gibson parade in October 1968 rolls by a vacant lot where his former residence once stood.

Gibson's signature season changed the game. He was still great the next four seasons, but never invincible.

"Everybody has his own definition of 'the good old days,' " Gibson wrote. "For me, they ended when the curtain was drawn on 1968."

For Marlin Briscoe, the rest of '68 was more complicated.

Had he started just one game, Briscoe might have gone down as a footnote. A failure. But he didn't go quietly to the bench. He recovered from Oct. 6 and shuffled back and forth with Denver's No. 1 quarterback.

On Oct. 27, Tensi threw his third interception of the day, prompting boos from the largest Broncos crowd in franchise history.

Trailing 14-0, Briscoe sparked a comeback, culminating with 1:55 left when he spotted an opening in the middle and audibled to a quarterback sneak. He squeezed through the defense untouched for the game-winning score.

"One of the most amazingly smart checkoff maneuvers I've ever seen," coach Saban said.

Afterward, the quarterback waited 20 minutes on the field for a TV interview. Impatient Broncos fans started chanting, "We want Briscoe." They "turned loose a thunderous salute," the Denver Post reported, as Marlin approached the south end zone, where his cousin, Bob Rose, had season tickets.

Briscoe earned AFL offensive player of the week. A month later, he finally got his second start. In the final minute against Buffalo, Briscoe rolled left and — just as the Saints scout described before the 1968 draft — heaved it more than 60 yards to a streaking receiver, setting up the game-winning field goal. Briscoe finished with 335 yards passing and four touchdowns.

Two weeks later, the day before Briscoe faced the Raiders, he got a phone call at the team hotel in Oakland.

This is your dad. Can I come see you?

For 23 years, Marlin knew his father only from Christmas gifts and birthday phone calls. Until that day, they'd never met. Marlin Sr. took his son to his neighborhood barbershop and pool hall. He introduced his friends.

"I looked just like him. Mom always said that."

The Raiders beat him the next day, but Briscoe made his mark in the final month. Chiefs coach Hank Stram called him "the most dangerous scrambling quarterback I've seen in nine years in the AFL. He's like playing against 12 men."

Briscoe started the final four games and threw for 10 touchdowns and 1,006 yards — more than Joe Namath, Len Dawson and Bob Griese during the same span. All of them became Hall of Fame quarterbacks. Briscoe never played the position again.

In '69, Denver moved Briscoe back to defense. He asked for his release and landed in Buffalo, where the Bills converted him to wide receiver.

Rule changes diminished Gibson. Stereotypes impeded Briscoe. Sayers suffered the most gruesome setback.

On Nov. 3, 1968, he rushed for a career-high 205 yards in a 13-10 win at Green Bay. His 824 yards and 6.5 yards per carry were on pace to shatter his career bests, too.

The following Sunday — five days after America elected Nixon to the White House — Sayers faced the same 49ers team on the same Wrigley Field where he scored six touchdowns as a rookie.

In the second quarter, Sayers swept right into a wall of defenders. Teammate Garry Lyle had blocked the play — "28 Toss, South Lin" — hundreds of times. Instinctively he waited for Sayers to cut back inside. Instead he heard Gale holler.

"I saw his eyes sort of glass over," Lyle said.

Just as Sayers planted his right leg in the grass, a San Francisco cornerback had crashed into him, bending the knee sideways. Teammates carried Sayers to the sideline, where a doctor bent over him and felt the knee. It's OK, he said, turning to walk away.

"Come back here!" Sayers screamed. "Tell it to me straight."

Doc finally told the truth. "The knee is gone, the ligaments are gone."

At halftime, football's human highlight reel left the field on a stretcher. And that night, Sayers endured a three-hour surgery.

In 1968, most players didn't come back at all from serious knee injuries. Sayers wasn't most players. He returned the following season and became a more hard-nosed runner. He led the NFL in rushing yards again, but his elusiveness was gone — his longest gain was just 28 yards.

A second knee injury a year later forced Sayers' retirement. He was 28 years old.

***

On Christmas Eve 1968, North Omaha kids lined up to see Black Santa Claus on 24th Street. They marveled at Edwin Donaldson's glistening lights on Corby Street. They shared dinner tables, gathered around trees and unwrapped the season's hottest toy, "Hot Wheels."

At 8:30 p.m., they took time out and turned their black-and-white TVs to the moon.

Until Apollo 8, no one had ever escaped Earth's gravitational field, let alone broadcast scenes from space.

That night, three American astronauts orbited the moon 60 miles above the surface — at 3,600 mph. They pointed a camera out their spacecraft window and gave 1 billion viewers a tour of a new world.

Thousands of impact craters. The Sea of Crises and Sea of Tranquility. Miles and miles of rocky desert.

"The best way to describe this is a vastness of black and white," astronaut William Anders told viewers. "Absolutely no color."

Before Apollo 8 escaped the moon's gravity trap and began its 49-hour journey home, the explorers fixed the camera on the lunar sunrise and took turns reading aloud.

Shhhh. Listen.

"In the beginning, God created the heaven and the Earth. And the Earth was without form and void; and darkness was upon the face of the deep. And the spirit of God moved upon the face of the waters. And God said, 'Let there be light.' And there was light. And God saw the light, that it was good; and God divided the light from the darkness."

A quarter of a million miles away, a neighborhood constrained by segregation's gravitational pull, devastated by economic decline and exhausted by social struggle inched closer to Christmas.

Clair Memorial church hosted an 11 p.m. candlelight service. Families bundled up and ventured into the 14-degree night as a crescent moon — the same one they'd just seen on their TVs — fell behind the clouds, lower and lower in the western sky.

At precisely 10:59, as believers climbed the church steps to sing carols, the sliver of light dropped below the horizon.

The new world above was gone. The old one beneath their feet wasn't coming back.

Chapter 11

Searching for Daylight

FROM TIME TO TIME, Roger Sayers finds the photograph and studies the marks that age can't erase. Two old men — great grandfathers — wearing the smiles of children.

The man in back, one day before his 72nd birthday, wraps his arms around big brother and clenches his hands together. The man in front, 73, flashes the same grin. He and Gale might as well be flying down Grant Street on homemade skateboards in 1955.

"A lot of folks say the older we get, the more we look like each other," Roger said.

In May 2015, Roger knew that Gale's memory was fading. He knew that Gale could be moody or disengaged, even non-responsive. But they were still brothers.

That week, Gale was in town and their alma mater, Central High, invited them downtown for a photo shoot. Gale drifted in and out. Lucid one minute, lost the next. At one point, a stranger got him chatting about old times and Gale thought about mom and dad. He broke down.

"Tears started flowing," Roger said.

Roger put a hand on his brother and eased him back to the moment. They started laughing and, seconds later, the photographer snapped the picture.

That's about the last time he remembers Gale being Gale.

Roger (front) and Gale Sayers at Central High on May 29, 2015.

A few days later, Roger woke up early and met his little brother in the kitchen. The morning was bright, the shadows long. "Good Morning America" played on TV.

Gale's wife, Ardie, was out of town. Roger's wife was still asleep. It was just the two of them sitting two feet apart at a table, just as they'd done thousands of times before.

Gale looked up and asked big brother a question. "Do you have Roger's telephone number?"

Roger looked at him, puzzled. "Yeah, what do you need it for?"

"Well, I want to call him because Ardie will be calling him. I want to make sure she knows that she needs to talk to me."

Roger swallowed hard. He paused. In a moment, he tried to wrap his arms around seven decades of shared memories. From Wichita to Speed to Omaha, where they bounced from house to house, leaning on each other when mom and dad couldn't hold them up.

From Howard Kennedy to Kountze Park to Central High to birthday parties and Christmases and golf outings and road trips and inside jokes, like Gale quitting his World-Herald paper route, leaving Roger to knock on doors and hopelessly ask for money. After all of that ... Gale really didn't know?

"I'll make sure that Roger has Ardie call you," Roger replied.

That was it. The rest of day, they watched TV and drove around Omaha and made small talk like strangers. All the while, Roger replayed the conversation at the breakfast table.

"I won't ever forget that moment," he says now. "I knew at that point things would not be right again."

The next time Roger saw Gale, he'd deteriorated dramatically.

So he keeps the picture handy. On his phone and on his computer. And when he thinks about the brother who hasn't recognized him in four years, the brother he hasn't seen in two years because it hurts too much, Roger opens the image and savors a bear hug and a smile.

He remembers. Because one of them has to.

***

On Jan. 6, 1969, a hero came home.

Bob Boozer's Chicago Bulls met Oscar Robertson's Cincinnati Royals at the jam-packed Civic Auditorium, a real regular-season NBA game (three years before the Kansas City-Omaha Kings era). Eighteen months after housing developers denied Boozer a place to live, he received a key to the city and a standing ovation. His 25 points weren't quite enough to beat the Big O.

As the '60s came to an end, sports hadn't lost its power in North Omaha, but the neighborhood had lost the infrastructure to develop the next generation.

High-paying labor jobs vanished. Black teens lost the freedom to roam and congregate. Trust in leaders and institutions collapsed — so did all sense of discipline. The men who experienced North Omaha's heyday watched its spirit shatter. Memory can't possibly gather and sort 50 years of that history, so the mind latches on to moments. Snapshots.

On June 24, 1969, police received a 10:25 p.m. call reporting a break-in at 1701 No. 21st St. The Logan Fontenelle projects. At the south unit of a brick apartment building, two cops detained a presumed burglar. They also spotted a 14-year-old girl fleeing the scene.

Vivian Strong lived at 1708, just across a narrow plaza from the crime scene. Friends said she had nothing to do with any robbery — she was merely dancing to records in the plaza — but years of friction between black kids and white cops prompted her to run.

Dressed in a white blouse and green shorts, she curled around an apartment building and ran down the alley as officer James Loder gave chase. When he spotted her about 100 feet away, Loder stopped and raised his revolver.

Vivian Strong

"Don't shoot!" a boy yelled behind him. "Don't shoot!"

The single bullet hit Vivian Strong in the back of the head.

Her 13-year-old sister ran to her body on the ground and looked at the cop: "Why?" Loder had no answer.

The California native and adopted son of movie star Hedy Lamarr had joined the Omaha police in 1966 after 8 ½ years in the Air Force. He was charged with manslaughter and released on a mere $500 bond, two facts that further enraged blacks.

To North Omaha, Strong's death wasn't just a tragedy, but a travesty. Since July 1966, police had killed four unarmed black teenagers.

At Strong's funeral on July 1, 1969, her mother, Kasie, sits left next to her father, James.

The Logan Fontenelle plaza between Vivian's home (left) and the site of the break-in (right).

Barber Dan Goodwin saw this one coming.

Four months earlier, he witnessed a speeding police cruiser screech its breaks outside Horace Mann Junior High, just in front of students getting off a school bus. A cop jumped out and pointed his revolver at kids. Goodwin reported the incident and wrote a letter to community leaders — he's kept a copy for 50 years. He also learned the officer's name: James Loder.

James Loder

The night after Strong's death, 1,000 people gathered on a baseball field in the projects, one of Josh Gibson's old practice diamonds. They distributed leaflets: "How many more black children have to be murdered by cops before something is done?"

Seven blocks north, 16-year-old Brenda Council hurried with friends from Bryant Center. Mom's shift at the VA hospital ended at 10 p.m. and Brenda couldn't be late. As she drove south down 24th Street, she saw the first flames off Decatur Street.

North 24th Street blanketed in smoke during the '69 riots.

She saw one of her basketball teammates running from Feldman's grocery, a ham tucked under her arm. Council turned west and crossed a police checkpoint at 30th Street.

"I gotta pick up my mom!"

Fifteen minutes later, she returned to the same intersection and the cops didn't bother her.

"They didn't care if you went in," Council said, "they just didn't want you to go out."

Police effectively contained the mayhem to North Omaha, but North 24th paid the price. For three nights, black rioters torched white-owned businesses — 17 total.

"They've called it the ghetto, the Near North Side, the poverty area, the slums," a World-Herald reporter wrote. "But if you were there Wednesday night and early today, you'd know it for what it was — an anteroom to Hell."

James Strong, Vivian's dad, pleaded for peace. "There are other ways to settle things without violence." But he couldn't stop it. The following night, city leaders deemed the area too dangerous for firemen. They just let it burn.

"I had tears in my eyes when I saw the places that Gibson and I loved so much get destroyed," Rodney Wead said. "It's hard to believe how rapid the decay was."

Firefighters douse the flames of a vacant home ablaze at 23rd and Clark Streets on the first night of riots following Strong's shooting.

In March 1970, an all-white jury exonerated 30-year-old James Loder of manslaughter, although the police department fired him a year later for other infractions. That August, the city's fraught relationship with North Omaha further deteriorated.

A 911 call at 2:07 a.m. reported a screaming woman being dragged into a house. Cops swarmed to 2867 Ohio St. As they searched the vacant house, a booby-trapped suitcase exploded at the doorway, killing officer Larry Minard. Two black men, David Rice and Edward Poindexter, were later convicted of murder and sentenced to life in prison.

Half a century later, those memories remain a source of horror and regret in North Omaha, especially Strong's death and the subsequent riots, the last major disturbance of the civil rights era. Vengeance blinded good judgment, pastor Alvin Mitchell said. Rioters didn't consider how the damage would diminish their ability to find a grocery store in 10 years. They didn't comprehend the civic backlash.

"After the riots," Cathy Hughes said, "Omaha was like, 'Well, you did it to your own neighborhood, live with it.' And they just left it."

But North Omaha's demise was always messier than abandoned lots.

On July 17, three weeks after the riots, the Nebraska Legislature's lone black senator, Ed Danner, finally captured his white whale — open housing. Lawmakers voted 38-6 to "prohibit discrimination in the sale, leasing and rental of property because of race, color, religion or national origin."

Open housing "won't erase all the scars of the past," Danner said, "but it may prevent further wounds."

Three days later, July 20, 1969, a billion viewers crowded around their TVs again and watched Neil Armstrong walk on the moon.

That's one small step for man, one giant leap for mankind.

Danner must have appreciated the symmetry. But he couldn't anticipate the devastating irony of a civil right he'd so valiantly pursued. Over the next two decades, the unintended consequences of open housing robbed North Omaha of its identity.

Danner didn't experience them. In January 1970, two weeks shy of his 70th birthday, he died of a heart attack. Who replaced the old packinghouse butcher and church deacon? A Creighton-educated atheist half his age.

Ernie Chambers.

Ernie Chambers and Dan Goodwin picket in protest of an OPS school board member.

***

His wife noticed changes in about 2009.

Gale traveled all the time for speeches and public appearances. Sometimes he neglected a minor detail. Or forgot a name. Or lost his train of thought. Ardie Sayers chalked it up to age. But the frequency increased.

"I'd tell him something and he'd say, you didn't tell me that."

Ardie's own memories go all the way back to South Omaha. If she takes a deep whiff, the 83-year-old can still smell the packinghouses where her father worked.

"We used to tease people. If they were in South Omaha, they'd say, 'Oh my God.' And we'd laugh, 'Oh, that's good for you. You'll get used to it.'"

In the '60s, Ardie joined the North Omaha YMCA board that included Roger Sayers. Ardie even helped care for Roger's mother before she died.

The only family member she didn't know? The famous one. Finally she met Gale at North Omaha's favorite cafe, the Fair Deal.

They tied the knot in 1973 — second marriages for both of them — and moved to Kansas where Gale worked in the KU athletic department. But they frequently

Ardie and Gale Sayers at the Omaha Press Club in 2004.

returned home to see family, especially during Native Omaha Days, the community reunion in North O every other summer. Once Gale even rode in the parade.

They eventually settled in rural Indiana and Gale launched a booming technology company. By 2012, he was semi-retired and spending a few months a year in Las Vegas, where he worked autograph conventions — he loved scribbling his name. In March, the whole family was in town when he abandoned his car at a red light and ran inside Walgreens. His nephew hurried to the driver's seat, parked the car and followed him inside.

"Uncle Gale, what are you doing?"

He had no clue.

Don Benning

Don Benning coached eight individual national champions at Omaha University.

The fieldhouse wrestling room resembled a Saharan attic. So small, so stifling that Omaha University wrestlers gravitated toward the door just to get a breath. But Don Benning didn't relent.

While the 1960s raged and his North Omaha neighborhood burned, Benning — the first black college coach at a predominantly white university — forged one of the nation's best college wrestling programs. At any level. Of course, it's easier to motivate when you're the toughest guy in the room.

"With all the champions we had, he could beat them all," former Omaha U. national champion Curlee Alexander said. "I never saw anybody walk in that room that could whoop Dr. Benning."

The coach grew up behind enemy lines. His house at 1334 Ogden St. sat in a poor, white neighborhood. Benning fought classmates everyday, routinely hearing a racial slur he described as "that word." Did he ever ask his parents to leave the neighborhood? "Obviously you don't know my father."

Dad hauled garbage. He retrieved bags. He worked at the packinghouse. Racial prejudice demoralized him. "My dad was a very ... very ... angry man. Sometimes he took that out on his family."

Don's isolation fueled an extraordinary sense of independence. Drive. "I said to myself, I'm going to do what I'm going to do, I don't care whether you like it or not."

At Omaha North, he won city titles in wrestling his junior and senior years then competed at Omaha U. in 1957-58, the first year the school offered the sport.

Benning wanted a teaching job, but OPS wasn't hiring black teachers. So in 1958, he packed his bags for Chicago. Then fate intervened. Benning stopped by Omaha U. to say a few good-byes, and the school president stopped him.

Milo Bail offered Benning a graduate fellowship in education. Five years later, Benning took over Omaha U. wrestling.

He endured slights and taunts. His team often clashed with officials and crowds — fans in North Carolina hung in effigy a dummy of UNO star Mel Washington. But as anger and hopelessness strangled North Omaha, Benning refused to waste his — or his team's — potential.

"You have to have a strong belief in self. I am somebody."

From 1968-71, the Indians were 55-3-2 in duals, including a win over vaunted Iowa. They won the NAIA national title in 1970.

A year later, Benning walked away to blaze new trails. First black doctorate recipient in NU's College of Education. First black athletic director in OPS. He led the district's desegregation effort and rose to assistant superintendent. Benning, who died in 2017 after a long battle with dementia, pinned to his office wall a poem that captured his tenacity. It concludes with this:

"Life's battles don't always go to the stronger or faster man; but sooner or later the man who wins is the one who thinks he can."

Charlie Washington

When Johnny Rodgers came down his stairs and saw the short, bald Irishman, his first impression of Bob Devaney wasn't pretty.

"The guy looked like Mr. Potato Head," Rodgers said.

North Omahans had said far worse things about Husker coaches. Through the 1950s and early '60s, Nebraska carried the image that it didn't embrace black athletes. Most of the neighborhood's best left the state for college, partly because they didn't feel welcome in Lincoln.

Devaney changed NU's reputation, but not without a little help from Charles Washington.

Nobody on the Near North Side had more credibility and connections than Washington, the Omaha Star journalist, activist and mentor. Washington interviewed President Johnson. He documented civil rights protests. He raised money for scholarship programs. He was "trusted on both sides of the fence," Rodgers said.

"Charlie was the hook-up guy," Rodgers said. "He was like the ghetto Godfather."

Of course, Devaney recognized influence and charm. He struck up a friendship with Washington that paid off in recruiting North Omaha athletes. Especially Rodgers.

In the winter of 1969, Nebraska was coming off back-to-back 6-4 seasons, and Rodgers had no interest in the Huskers. He eyed the bright lights of Los Angeles — USC and UCLA.

But Washington encouraged the Tech superstar to meet the Nebraska coach. He set up Devaney's visit to Rodgers' house. Johnny eventually got past the coach's appearance and recognized his skill and persistence.

"Every day, I went into the locker room, there was Bob Devaney," Tech basketball assistant John Morse said. "I don't know how many days he spent recruiting Johnny."

Rodgers signed with NU and ignited Devaney's back-to-back national titles. But Washington's importance extended beyond matchmaking.

He gave Devaney's out-of-state black players a home away from home.

In '68, Washington bought Bob Boozer's old place on Erskine Street and began hosting gatherings. "He had a very small house," Rodgers said, that seemed smaller yet when packed with defensive linemen like Rich Glover.

One night, Brenda Council — still in high school — arrived at a party at Washington's and met Huskers Willie Harper and Daryl White.

"These were the biggest guys I'd ever seen in my life," Council said.

In September 1976 — 10 years before his death — Washington's "celebrity roast" at Peony Park attracted a crowd of 600 people and 30 joke-tellers, including Bob Boozer, Bob Gibson, Roger Sayers, Rodney Wead and a short, bald Irishman.

Mr. Potato Head.

When Devaney took the microphone, tongue planted firmly in cheek, he credited his old friend for his coaching success.

"Charlie and I had to get the best athletes money could buy. So I came to Omaha and got Mike Green, Dick Davis and Johnny Rodgers."

Then the punchline.

"Johnny took a cut when he went into pro football."

The champions' locker room reeked of Champagne, spraying Oscar Robertson's jersey and Kareem Abdul-Jabbar's Afro and the 34-year-old face of Bob Boozer, who smiled in front of a national TV camera.

"I just want to say hello to all my friends in Omaha."

In the spring of 1971, Boozer capped his NBA career with a ring in Milwaukee, and Ron Boone captured an ABA title in Utah. That fall in Lincoln, Johnny Rodgers tore the Oklahoma Sooners loose from their shoes en route to Nebraska's second straight national title.

It was a banner year for Tech sports alums. And a terrible year for Tech students. Across the school district, blacks clashed with authority.

New state senator Ernie Chambers sought to outlaw corporal punishment, criticizing black administrators at Horace Mann for paddling students. At Franklin School, black

Three weeks before Johnny Rodgers (left) won his second national championship, Rodney Wead honored him at the Wesley House.

parents accused teachers of brutalizing and humiliating students, even giving them depressants. But the mayhem centered at 33rd and Cuming Streets. Tech High and Junior High — Vivian Strong's old school — occupied the district's largest building, but even at 50 percent capacity, everyone needed more space. You could feel rage just walking down the halls.

"Overnight, we went from acting like 14-year-olds before Vivian Strong's death to acting like 40-year-old revolutionaries," said Franklin Thompson, former Tech student.

Principal Carl Palmquist, the face of Tech for two decades, resigned from weariness in '71, opening the job for Odra Bradley, the first black OPS principal. Conditions declined.

"We had demonstrations," administrative assistant John Crookham said later. "We had marches. We had sit-ins. We had walk-arounds. We had everything except school that year."

Carol Strong, Vivian's little sister, accused two boys of pulling a knife and cutting her cheek. Police arrested an 18-year-old senior for raping a 13-year-old middle schooler. A woman standing at Tech's main entrance was robbed at gunpoint. A cafeteria protest led to flipped tables, broken windows and a canceled day of school. Madness even spilled over to Friday nights.

A referee ejected a Tech High basketball player for throwing a punch at a Council Bluffs Thomas Jefferson opponent. Then the player went after the official. Tech students emptied the stands and one fan punched the ref above the eye.

Chambers called the conditions at Tech deplorable. "If you want revolutionaries, let Tech High be destroyed," he told the Legislature. "This is the school my people attend."

He also encouraged kids to resist violence and develop their minds. "School is not a game," Chambers told a Tech High assembly in January 1972. "We're in a life and death struggle in this country. You have to understand it and take your part to overcome it."

That word — overcome — used to inspire and empower the black community. But kids lost faith that resilience made any difference. In August 1971, 356 Tech seniors started the school year. Nine months later, only 159 graduated. Racism and the ghetto "ate us up," said Thompson, one of the graduates, now Omaha Director of Human Rights and Relations.

Once a community anchor, Tech fell on hard times.

Roger Sayers, head of the Urban League in the late-'70s, recalled a generational shift born out of the '60s. Free will. "You couldn't tell me no," Sayers said. "If you told me no, you had to tell me why."

When Sayers entered OPS classrooms and tried to motivate students, they were too busy talking among themselves.

"I stopped going to schools," Sayers said. "It was just a waste of time. There was no discipline in the classroom."

Community criticism of Tech focused on its curriculum, deemed outdated by many leaders and parents. The economy trended toward white-collar jobs and blacks perceived vocational classes as an insult. OPS didn't help Tech's reputation, funneling behavioral and special-ed students there.

"It had become pretty much a dumping ground," recalled Sam Crawford, the junior high principal. "Kids that had any kind of intellectual capacity were not going to Tech."

Even the "Committee for the Future of Tech High School" recommended closing: "The consensus was that we now are (a school for special education) except in name."

Meanwhile, white families looked for ways out. Tech High was 17 percent black when Boozer entered in 1951. Blacks became the majority in Fred Hare's senior year, 1963. A decade later, only 22 white students remained, even though Tech was in a majority-white neighborhood.

Why?

Tech, unlike most district schools, allowed students to option out. And whites did.
In one year alone, 103 white students obtained transfers out of Tech Junior High. In '73,
the U.S. Department of Justice accused OPS of racial discrimination.

One year later, Tech High's enrollment dropped to 503 in a building that once housed almost 3,700. The future looked so ominous
that OPS briefly shuttered Tech football and basketball programs
before an uproar changed their minds.

When a federal court mandated busing in '76, Tech got an enrollment bump. But it didn't last. Increasing white flight and declining
district enrollment led to Tech High's end in 1984. Once the pride
of North Omaha, it became home to OPS offices.

"Certainly I have a feeling of remorse," Boozer said upon Tech's
closing. "It produced more outstanding athletes than any other
school."

Josh Gibson, age 60.

If anyone had the sheer will to save Tech High, it was Josh Gibson (class of '39). But the catalyst for Omaha's greatest generation of athletes drifted into the neighborhood background
in the '70s as his family dismantled. Divorced from his wife and estranged from his kids, Josh
found a new routine, working in social services.

In 1981, the Baseball Hall of Fame inducted his little brother. Since the mid-'60s, Josh and
Bob drifted apart and it didn't improve with Bob's retirement. Little brother paid his sisters'
way to Cooperstown for the ceremony, but his brothers were on their own. Josh refused to go.

On Sept. 21, 1982, the last official day of summer, Josh drove a friend home from work. He
walked back to his car on North 18th Street when he suffered a heart attack and died. He was 61.

Zion Baptist hosted the funeral and a big crowd attended. But when the service ended,
nephew Fred Jr. said, they realized they didn't have enough pallbearers — Josh was a big man.
The Gibsons rushed to the casket and lifted. Even Bob.

"We all put that man in the hearse," Fred Jr. said.

Josh's former players took it hard. Phil Wise, a '67 Tech High grad and NFL safety, lost his
dad at 12 years old, just about the time he came under Josh's wing. Sixty years later, he better
understands the men who blazed trails, sometimes with great personal sacrifice.

"They were in the fire. Discrimination burning all around. Every turn, nobody was there to
help them. And sometimes it gets the best of you. You're just mean. You don't trust. Those
demons still follow us around. Josh had those demons. Look at what Bob Gibson has accomplished; those demons still follow him. If you're a black man and you grew up through those
times, we all faced those demons."

Wise keeps a wall hanging in his TV room: "I can do hard things." That's what Josh Gibson
represented to him.

"If it's hard, it's worth something."

The next Gibson

Blackhawks Head to Regional —World-Herald Photo.

Since Bob Gibson retired from baseball in 1975, his hometown has produced precisely one black major leaguer: Kimera Bartee (1996-2001). And according to a mostly retired collection of black administrators, teachers and coaches, the blame falls on them.

"We dropped the ball," says Jerry Bartee, Creighton's head coach in the '70s and Kimera's father. "What we said all along is when we got through, we'd get a huge program built. We talked about it. We talked about it. And talked about it."

"We got too busy," says Sam Crawford, former Tech Junior High principal.

Bartee and Crawford, along with guys like William Reed and Gene Haynes, are former teammates on North Omaha's finest men's softball team, the Blackhawks. Once a month they meet for lunch, mostly to tease each other. Occasionally, though, they sink their teeth into something real. Like the legacy of Josh Gibson and the decline of black baseball.

Jerry Bartee envisions a viable black baseball academy in Omaha that teaches the love of the game, not just winning. It would take churches, schools and rec centers to coordinate. It would take time.

"Six people sitting around this table right now," Bartee told his friends one day in 2018, "if we wanted to, we could get it done. We don't got to go no place to talk about funding. We can reach in our pockets for what it takes to get something started" — Bartee pounds the table — "and we got enough connections that we could go to people and say, 'Hey look, can you help us?'

"If Jerry Bartee would get his ass off the golf course and devote this time. And I know I worked 30-plus years to put myself in position to golf and fish and do what I want. But we didn't give back like we said we would! To the kids! We didn't! We've had this conversation before."

"Fifteen years ago!" Crawford says.

Of course, they overlook a critical component of Josh Gibson's success — a captive audience. He lived in the neighborhood; so did his players. "We're scattered all over town now," Al Gilmore says. And they're 65-plus years old. By that age, Josh was dead.

Soon the Blackhawks are teasing each other again about suburban life and riding lawnmowers, acreages near Fort Calhoun and cabins by Wahoo.

"Shut up, Mr. Beaver Lake," Bartee says.

"Who else can wake up in the morning and watch the deer?" Gilmore says.

A few days later, Crawford reflected on the lunch discussion. His friends didn't address one piece of this problem, he said. The risk of rejection and failure. For 50 years, North Omaha has a bad batting average. Do you want to spend your retired years swinging at pitches you can't hit?

Men like Charles Washington, Ernie Chambers and Rodney Wead were giants in the neighborhood. But 20 years later, Crawford said, "you look back and say, man, did they make a difference? Those guys busted their butt and went through all kinds of stuff.

"North Omaha is the same or worse than it was before they made their effort."

Every year, Gale Sayers traveled to the Mayo Clinic for his physical. By 2013, Ardie feared something was terribly wrong.

She detailed his symptoms, prompting a series of tests that led to a diagnosis: dementia. Doctors believed that football played a major role.

The goal line moved that day. The daily routine didn't change. "For better or worse, for richer or poorer," Ardie says. "You're supposed to stay together and go through it together."

Trials tested their patience. Gale didn't take orders easily, especially from strangers. *Get away from me!* Now he has a nurse in the home 24 hours a day. He can't sign his name. He can't brush his teeth. Often he can't feed himself.

He once said he needed only "18 inches of daylight" to elude a defense. Now Galloping Gale is trying to walk again.

He attends physical therapy three times a week, but he spends his days in a modified wheelchair, usually hunched over. When he rocks back and forth, Ardie knows what he wants. But if he gets up unattended, surely he'll fall. In May 2019, he crashed before she could reach him, leaving a cut on his head.

"It's tough when you look at a person and see what they used to be and how they've changed," she says.

Through it all, Ardie wonders ... what does he remember?

Memorabilia lines the walls. Footballs and photos of Gale's career. Ardie opens albums and points out his kids and friends. She goes over the names. Every once in a while, a flicker of daylight appears. Hope dashes into the room like Gale through a defense.

A friend tells a story and Gale laughs. Or a nurse inserts a DVD of his playing days and marvels at the way he weaves through tacklers. "Gale," she says, "you were really fast, weren't you?"

"Yes."

Ardie hears a word and cheers. "Yay!"

When Earl Campbell calls, his voice is so distinctive that Gale perks up. When Dick Butkus phoned the day before Gale's 76th birthday — I'm calling you early, buddy — Gale lit up. "He even chuckled," Ardie said.

In June, Gale's nephew — Roger's oldest son — arrived from Hawaii. He walked in and found Gale curled over in his chair. He kissed his uncle on the head and began greeting others in the house. That's when Raymond felt a bear hug from behind. *Uncle Gale? Uncle Gale!*

It's almost like he's in a shell, Raymond says.

"You know when you're telling somebody a story and you're trying to recall a name and it's on the tip of your tongue and you see it, you know it, but you can't get it out? I think that's him all the time. And that's the reason why he doesn't speak.

"He's in there. You know he's in there. But there's no vocabulary."

The outdoor courts looked the same, but only memories occupied them.

Ron Boone came home in the summer from from Salt Lake City and returned to his basketball "haven" at Bryant Center. In his day, bouncing balls and trash talk and cheering spectators gave the place a rhythm. A soundtrack. By the '80s, Boone heard only silence.

From 1960-80, the number of businesses along the four blocks of 24th Street south of Lake had dropped from 52 to 15. Chambers compared North 24th to a "collapsed artery."

Coach Gene Haynes and Tech High honored alum Ron Boone upon his NBA retirement in 1980.

Every man has his metaphor.

In the mid-'50s, Chambers and Bob Gibson enrolled in the same Spanish class at Creighton. The future state senator watched the future Hall of Fame pitcher weave together a long cord hanging from the window shade. That's how Chambers learned to braid.

"You make the first loop," Chambers said. "Then you pull the next one down through it, then the next one through that and when you got through, that cord was not two individual strings that looped at the bottom, it was a chain."

At its best, North Omaha braided its strands beautifully. But the '60s tugged at a few, the '70s pulled a few more. By the '80s, the chain unraveled.

"In basic needs — education, employment, shelter, nutrition, health care — this community as a whole is worse off than it ever was," Chambers said then.

Gibson invested in numerous North Omaha businesses, including the radio station, KOWH. But blacks didn't have sponsorship dollars and when he approached white businesses, Gibson felt like he was pitching uphill. Take his friend, a tire distributor.

"He had the gall to tell me black people don't buy tires," Gibson said. "For the life of me, how in the hell am I going to get people to buy (ads) when they have that mindset?"

North Omaha's commercial collapse paralleled a plummeting housing stock. Freeway construction and home condemnations reduced the number of homes in 20 years from 8,900 to 4,900. In 1960, the Near North Side counted almost 30,000 residents. By '80, it dropped to 10,900.

Where did all those people go? Some to Denver or Kansas City. Some to Chicago or Los Angeles. Even more to Atlanta and the South, reversing the Great Migrations. There's a reason Native Omaha Days became such a big deal, Preston Love Jr. says. "Because everybody left."

Of those who stayed in Nebraska, the most successful often moved to Bellevue, Benson or west Omaha. By '83, about 25 percent of the city's 40,000 black residents lived in the old neighborhood, compared to 82 percent in 1960.

William Reed

Open housing righted a moral wrong and opened new opportunities, but it fractured black unity and cohesion. No longer did doctors, lawyers and accountants live next to factory workers.

During the civil rights era, former Central High football coach William Reed said, the neighborhood resembled "a big glass ball that was slowly falling to the surface." Rich or poor, prominent or ordinary, blacks were stuck inside.

"That thing hit the ground and shattered all over the place. There's some big chunks that came out and some smaller chunks that stayed in. They were destined to never be together again."

The crash resembles brain drain in rural America. Once upon a time, North Omaha was good enough for everybody. Suddenly, it wasn't. Here comes the unintended consequences:

Dilution of black culture and political power. Accumulation of resentment and bitterness from those who couldn't leave the neighborhood. Disinvestment in the community. You spend your money where you live, multi-millionaire Cathy Hughes said, not where you grew up.

"Integration was the worst enemy of black economic development because no longer were you forced to go to the black doctor or shop at the black store," Hughes said. "Because you had a choice. And because you had been deprived for so long, the choice you exercised was often times to the detriment of the black community. We didn't realize that. No one told us."

Think of the problem from the perspective of a black teenager in the Logan Fontenelle projects in the 1980s. Before integration, if a kid wanted to be a doctor, Eric Ewing said, his mom could send him to talk to the doctor across the street. Now those mentors reside elsewhere.

"If you can't see those things, you can't even imagine those things," said Ewing, executive director of the Great Plains Black History Museum. "We went from a 5-star menu of life choices down to a McDonald's menu of burgers and fries."

Bob Gibson and Bob Boozer grew up half a mile apart, just a brisk walk down 24th Street. By the '80s, Gibson lived 10 miles south; Boozer 13 miles west.

Omaha still produced accomplished black athletes: Mike McGee, Larry Station, Maurtice Ivy, Ron Kellogg, Kerry Trotter, Erick Strickland, Andre Woolridge, Ahman Green. But they weren't as frequent, weren't as spectacular and likely didn't gain as much strength from their environment.

Segregation, horrific as it was, forced young black athletes to compete against each other; they couldn't just transfer to Bellevue or Millard for more playing time. Discrimination, repugnant as it was, bonded those athletes at Kountze Park and Bryant Center.

Love, the ex-Husker end, compared it to a football team. "I would fight with teammates at Nebraska, but when we played Oklahoma, we locked arms and kicked ass. This community locked arms in some sort of mental way that brought us together. ...

"It was magic."

Perhaps dispersion and dilution were inevitable. Black professionals wanted newer homes, better schools and safer streets, just like whites did. But Love Jr. says the goal should've been desegregation, not integration. Knock down the walls of discrimination to create equal opportunities. But don't leave.

"Just build a better house down here in North Omaha."

The sales pitch got even tougher in 1987 when Los Angeles-based street gangs, Bloods and Crips, arrived in North Omaha and took over Love's childhood paradise, the Logan Fontenelle projects. Once hailed a "Cinderella transformation," Omaha's first housing project developed a new nickname: "Vietnam." Twenty-second and Charles, the same intersection Josh and Bob Gibson overlooked in 1947 when they sat on the front step and talked life and baseball, became ground zero for drug trafficking. Crack Corner.

Even former Logan residents like Rodney Wead argued to raze the whole complex and start over. Before he moved to St. Louis in '92, Wead — who owned a doctorate in sociology — examined the epidemic of poverty, unemployment and mass incarceration. "Black men," Wead said in '92, "are becoming an endangered species."

A few years later, his childhood best friend decided to take a drive. Bob Gibson doesn't remember the year. At age 83, they all run together. He left his Bellevue home and rolled north through downtown, past his alma maters, Kellom, Tech High and Creighton. At Paul Street, Gibson should've seen the brick buildings that shaped his life. Logan Fontenelle.

"It was just gone."

The basketball courts where the Gibson brothers took on all competition. Gone. The long sidewalks where his friends raced. Gone. The rec center at 22nd and Clark Streets that Marty Thomas turned into a haunted house on Halloween and a movie theater on Friday nights — Buster Crabbe B-Westerns! — and occasionally his own personal kitchen, dumping his gunny sack of crawdads he caught from Carter Lake with liver bait and bamboo poles and boiling them in a large pot. That gym stunk for a week!

"Guess what?" Gibson said. "It's not there. I don't even know where that building was anymore."

In Logan Fontenelle's place, Gibson saw a neighborhood of new houses, like something he'd see in Bellevue. Kids making new memories in places maybe they'll remember in 50 years.

"Time passes so fast."

He tipped his hat to progress, turned his car south back to Bellevue and returned to the only home he knew.

Ardie pulled his large gold blazer from the closet and waited for the limousine.

For months, the Chicago Bears coaxed the Sayers family to participate in its 100th anniversary celebration. For weeks, Ardie deliberated if Gale could handle the crowds. Finally, she said yes to one more public appearance. "Let him smell the roses while he's still alive."

Friends and family flew in to lend a hand. Gale's nurses and physical therapists prepared him. On June 7, 2019, his entourage made the 130-mile trip from Wakarusa, Indiana, to Chicago. Gale still loves car rides, often pointing out animals on the side of the road — or just pointing his driver which way he wants to go.

When they pulled up to Rosemont Convention Center, the train of limos looked like a scene from Hollywood. A stranger came up from the car behind and knocked on their window.

"You guys gotta get out of the way. We have (former all-pro lineman) Revie Sorey!"

"I got Gale Sayers," the driver said.

"Oh."

Gale's nephew pushed him inside via wheelchair, where current Bears gathered around Sayers like little kids around a teacher. They weren't sure what to do next. Can we shake his hand, a defensive back asked. Raymond Sayers nodded and the DB felt Gale's squeeze.

"Man, he's strong."

Bears coaches greeted him. The franchise owner, too. But Gale didn't lift his eyes. And Raymond worried this whole mission might be a mistake.

For years, fans walked up to Sayers at restaurants, sometimes intrusively, requesting autographs or pictures. Why do you accommodate them, his family asked. Gale's response: You don't know how far they've come and how long they waited to meet you. Don't spoil their moment.

Now Raymond stood behind his uncle hoping the family hadn't asked for too much. Would the crowd wonder if Gale was even awake?

They rolled down a long hallway and waited next to Butkus, who expressed sadness that his friend had declined further since their last visit. In front of the curtain, the crowd welcomed all the prominent Bears, decade by decade. Louder and louder.

Behind the curtain, Gale's time was coming.

That's when Raymond looked down and remembered a scene from his childhood. A flashback to a time when Gale Sayers mesmerized football fans across the country. Just before returning kickoffs, he executed his little ritual. A method to get his blood flowing.

Now, moments from hearing his name, Gale did it again. He rubbed his hands together. Back and forth. Back and forth.

"Right on, uncle! Let's go!"

From behind the curtain, his nephew rolled Gale into an arena of blinding spotlights and boisterous strangers.

Searching for Daylight

Gale Sayers at the Bears 100 celebration in June 2019.

At 130 pounds, his Hall of Fame jacket didn't fit anymore. Two straps — one across his waist, one across his feet — constrained him in the wheelchair. His bony knees, scarred by surgeries, pressed against each other. But he kept his head up. He saw the standing ovation. He heard the roar. And for a few moments, Gale Sayers must have felt the embrace of 9,000 friends.

A bear hug.

Without word or expression, he raised his left hand to his face and wiped his eye.

***

He broke his foot playing racquetball. Then he dislocated his shoulder playing softball. That's after two knee replacements. These days The Jet could use a propeller. But Johnny Rodgers' spirit? Never better.

It's a splendid summer day in 2019 and North Omaha's chief ambassador, dressed in jeans, sport coat and red pocket square, walks the street of his past. Present, too.

"Hey, Johnny!" a driver calls out as the '72 Heisman Trophy winner crosses 24th Street in front of Bryant Center. Rodgers laughs. "I think I'm more popular now than I used to be."

Boozer died of a brain aneurysm in 2012. Gibson and Roger Sayers live in the suburbs. Boone, Marlin Briscoe and Gale Sayers live far away. Down here, Johnny's the only one left.

"That's where I had my first job," Rodgers says, pointing at The Omaha Star. "Selling newspapers." And this building, the Great Plains Black History Museum, is where he sometimes displays his Heisman.

When Rodgers moved home from San Diego in the early '90s, Johnny vowed he'd never live west of 72nd Street. Turns out he stayed east of 24th. He bought a 1935 house on Wirt Street, added a hot tub and anchored his neighborhood in sickness and in health.

Finally, after 50 years, Rodgers senses a rebirth.

Blueprints detail multi-million dollar development projects. Othello Meadows, a 1994 all-state basketball player at Creighton Prep who practiced law in Atlanta before returning home, leads a revitalization group, "Seventy Five North," that has modernized North 30th Street with mixed-income housing and splashy new buildings like "The Venue."

On the east side of the freeway, the Goodwin family pushes revitalization of North 24th, where the Spencer Street Barber Shop still flourishes. Twenty years after Dan's son and daughter-in-law moved to northwest Omaha, they're packing boxes and coming back.

Cathy Hughes

"I belong here," LaVonya Goodwin says. "And I feel like it's my responsibility. But it's not a burden, it's a call."

Rodgers nurtures his own development partnerships with native Omahans like Cathy Hughes. "You can do a Midtown Crossing and call it the 24th Street Crossing," says Hughes, the founder of Urban One in Washington D.C. "I feel hope."

It isn't just commerce. The Sacred Heart school that kept out blacks in 1950? Now it leads one of North Omaha's most aggressive community outreach programs. Its school is 99 percent black. The City Council that once thwarted an open housing ordinance appointed in 2015 a black president. The school district that once shunned black high school teachers now has a black superintendent.

One of the world's best prizefighters, Bud Crawford, wears "Omaha" across his boxing trunks.

Still, poverty cripples much of the neighborhood, including Pinkney Street, where the home of Johnny's grandparents stood before the freeway erased it. His neighbors Jerry Bartee and Brenda Council observed the breakdown of families and yearn for the lively front porches of their childhood. "We gotta get back to the Pinkney Street of the '50s and '60s," Council said.

For numerous reasons, the task is daunting. A century after Will Brown and 50 years after Vivian Strong, Ernie Chambers, who's spent more time in the Legislature than any Nebraskan in history, sees a racist system that evolves, but rarely changes.

"It's not Jim Crow. It's Mr. James Crow, Esq.," said Chambers, 81. "The Ku Klux Klan takes off the pillow cases and bed sheets and they wear Brooks Bros. suits and homburg hats."

Skepticism persists on 24th Street, too. When John Beasley drives past the corners where he harmonized with his buddies and bought comic books, he sees ghosts. "It'll never be what it was. Those days are gone. And if it is rejuvenated, it will probably be gentrification."

But Rodgers, 67, sees a world where the future and past can co-exist. At 24th and Burdette, Skeet's barbecue still occupies the east side of the road. Same sign as 60 years ago! But on the west side, where the Fair Deal once thrived, sits the new Emery's Cafe.

Johnny walks in and finds a table next to the patio. Every few minutes, his phone rings.

He works for the Census Bureau to make sure blacks get counted in 2020 — "there's dollars in the data." He heads new leadership groups like 100 Black Men and Black Knights — "I got a whole group of people working together now that never even talked to each other before." He chases 10 grandkids, mentors troubled kids one-on-one, helps his neighborhood association...

Which reminds him, Rodgers picks up his phone, makes a call and checks what time he needs to help set up at tomorrow's picnic.

Like his peers, Rodgers laments North Omaha's demise. Good jobs mean everything, he says. When the trades and packinghouse jobs disappeared, guys started self-medicating, which leads to low self-esteem and shame. Pretty soon you're pulling down your neighbors instead of lifting them up.

He wants a new generation of welders, plumbers and electricians. "You can make as much money as a doctor — with no student loan debt." He wants blacks keeping their money in the community. He wants this old corridor to look like modern-day *South* Omaha. A business on every corner.

"This is the most valuable land in Omaha. It's close to downtown, midtown, the airport." People try to denigrate the area, Rodgers says, but it's more attractive than 144th out west. "They don't have no trees. We got trees!"

You really think it's coming back, Johnny?

"It's already happening! The College World Series is on Cuming Street!"

***

Every night, Gale Sayers stiff arms the darkness.

And every morning, Ardie asks God for a few more inches of daylight. *Watch out for him. Help him endure.* Then she goes to her husband of 46 years and says: "OK, the Lord let us wake up another day. Let's make the best of it."

And sometimes Gale gives her a sound — a confirmation.

Ardie thinks the Bears 100 celebration did him good. "I was so proud of him." The experience gave her hope that Gale might be up for one more road trip. This time, all the way home. Native Omaha Days.

Maybe it's just a dream. Maybe it's asking too much. But if it's hard, it's worth something.

She envisions all of North Omaha, past and present, in one place for one weekend. Picnics and reunions, music and dances, jokes about packinghouse smells and greasy Ritz popcorn.

She envisions a parade. Thousands of people on both sides of the street. A line of cars stretching as far as she can see. Sports cars and clown cars, midget football teams and drill teams, fraternities and sororities, parents camped out in lawn chairs and kids stuffing plastic bags full of candy.

The old generation would be there. Rodney Wead, Preston Love Jr., Cathy Hughes, John Beasley, Brenda Council, Jerry Bartee, Dan Goodwin, Chambers in his short-sleeve sweatshirt, even Ella Boozer, who lives in the same west Omaha house her late husband bought in 1968. All the faces — famous and unheralded — who cherish the heritage of North Omaha. And their kids, grandkids and great-grandkids would surround them, hoping it's not too late to share.

At the end of the parade, in a string of convertibles ushered by drum lines, here comes Omaha's greatest generation of athletes.

There's Bob Gibson, just up the hill from the Kellom schoolyard where he learned to pitch in 1947, battling pancreatic cancer as fiercely as he did the Detroit Tigers. And Marlin Briscoe, across town from his old birch tree, marveling at all the little quarterbacks in the crowd.

There's Ron Boone, cradling his basketball, itching for a 3-on-3 game at Bryant Center. And Johnny Rodgers, smiling at his Wirt Street neighbors as he flashes his Heisman pose.

"A couple of 'em," Ardie says, "could even ride together."

Maybe that's the last car. Gale and Roger Sayers. Growing up, they knew every corner of North Omaha. They ran circles around kids from 30th Street to Kountze Park. They proved that the strongest family is a tight community.

As their car passes by and the parade rolls down the hill, wrap your arms around the scene. Savor the cheers. Absorb the drumbeats bouncing off the street and echoing through the trees, whispering a truth too painful and too glorious to forget.

This neighborhood, once confined by hate, produced a story no longer confined by time.

A story destined to outlive its heroes.

Searching for Daylight

INDEX

Index

ACKNOWLEDGEMENTS

This project started way back in 2006.

I was a second-year World-Herald reporter researching Marlin Briscoe, who had recently appeared in a Nike commercial. Finally, "The Magician" had received a little national acclaim for being pro football's first black starting quarterback.

Dirk Chatelain

Briscoe's feat fascinated me because of its time period. So I started researching Omaha's other prominent black athletes of the era: Bob Gibson, Gale Sayers, Bob Boozer, Johnny Rodgers. What were they doing on Oct. 6, 1968? That's when the lightning bolt hit me.

I was hooked!

By early 2009, I'd interviewed most of the main characters and recognized that the real story wasn't the extraordinary athletes, it was the place they came from. But converting that idea to a full narrative was daunting. Rather than push through, I found other subjects. I put my North Omaha files on the shelf. I gave up.

In August 2018, after years of kicking myself, I determined the project was now or never. Now I'm more than a decade behind schedule, but I'm convinced the timing is right.

"24th and Glory" took off because of fascinating sources who devoted considerable time and energy for no personal gain. I conducted extensive interviews with more than 60 characters. Among the most valuable: Marlin Briscoe, Roger Sayers, Johnny Rodgers, Bob Gibson, Ron Boone, John Beasley, Brenda Council, Preston Love Jr., Cathy Hughes, Jerry Bartee, William Reed, Sam Crawford, Dan Goodwin, Ernie Chambers and one of the wisest men I've ever known, Rodney Wead, who saw this story long before I did. I regret that Bob Boozer, Don Benning and Bob Rodgers, whom I interviewed before their deaths, didn't see this project complete. I hope it honors them.

"24th and Glory" got a boost from excellent secondary sources, including the athletes' autobiographies, Omaha historical books and academic theses. (A thorough list of references can be found at Omaha. com/glory). A special thanks goes out to local authors who previously examined North Omaha, especially Adam Fletcher Sasse, Leo Adam Biga, John Dechant and Steve Marantz. This project had no chance without essential detail and context provided by The World-Herald and The Omaha Star digital archives. The city's 1950s and '60s reporters documented local history on deadline with superb craft and judgment. Hopefully, Omaha journalists 50 years from now will say the same about our generation.

"24th and Glory" reached the finish line because of colleagues whose good nature somehow exceeds their incredible talent and work ethic. Each has a distinct skill set, but so many were indispensable: Thad Livingston, Paul Goodsell, Hunter Paniagua, Graham Archer, Matt Haney, Tammy Yttri, Christine Zueck-Watkins and Kristine Gerber. For months, they poured their hearts and minds into this project; I'm so blessed to be on their team.

Finally, I want to thank my kids — Luke, Natalie and Calvin — who will be forced to read this book someday, and my wife, Andrea, who surely got tired of my shame and self-pity (my best qualities!) as I stared at blank computer screens. She tolerated my late nights at the table squinting at 1950s news articles. She brainstormed ideas. She edited chapters. She even contributed to the book title and the last paragraph. Writing is hard (at least for me) and Andrea is my muse — and my best friend.

PHOTOGRAPHY CREDITS

ABOUT THE AUTHOR

Dirk Chatelain is a lifelong Nebraskan. A native of Rising City (population 392), he graduated from Columbus High School and the University of Nebraska-Lincoln and now resides in Gretna. A five-time Nebraska sportswriter of the year, his journalism career includes 18 Associated Press Sports Editor Top-10 awards. "24th & Glory" is his first book project.

EDITORS
Kristine Gerber
Paul Goodsell
Thad Livingston
Hunter Paniagua

DESIGNER
Christine Zueck-Watkins

ILLUSTRATOR
Matt Haney

COPY EDITOR
Pam Richter

MARKETING
Rhonda Gray
Michelle Gullett
Rich Warren
Joshua Kellams

A product of the Omaha World-Herald

Todd Sears
Publisher

Melissa Matczak
Executive Editor

Copies of the book are available at www.owhstore.com.

Discounts are available for bulk orders.

For more information call 402-444-1014.

Bob Gibson, Marlin Briscoe, Johnny Rodgers and Ron Boone at the Baxter Arena in 2016.